ZOO

This book is dedicated to my father and mother.

Phaidon Press Limited
Regent's Wharf
All Saints Street
London N1 9PA

First published 1996
© 1996 Phaidon Press Limited

Britta Jaschinski would like to thank Peter Searle
for his help with the text.

ISBN 0 7148 3472 6

A CIP catalogue record for this book
is available from the British Library.

All rights reserved. No part of this publication
may be reproduced, stored in a retrieval
system or transmitted, in any form or by any
means, electronic, mechanical, photocopying,
recording or otherwise, without the prior
permission of Phaidon Press Limited.

Printed in Hong Kong

Britta Jaschinski **ZOO**

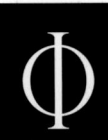

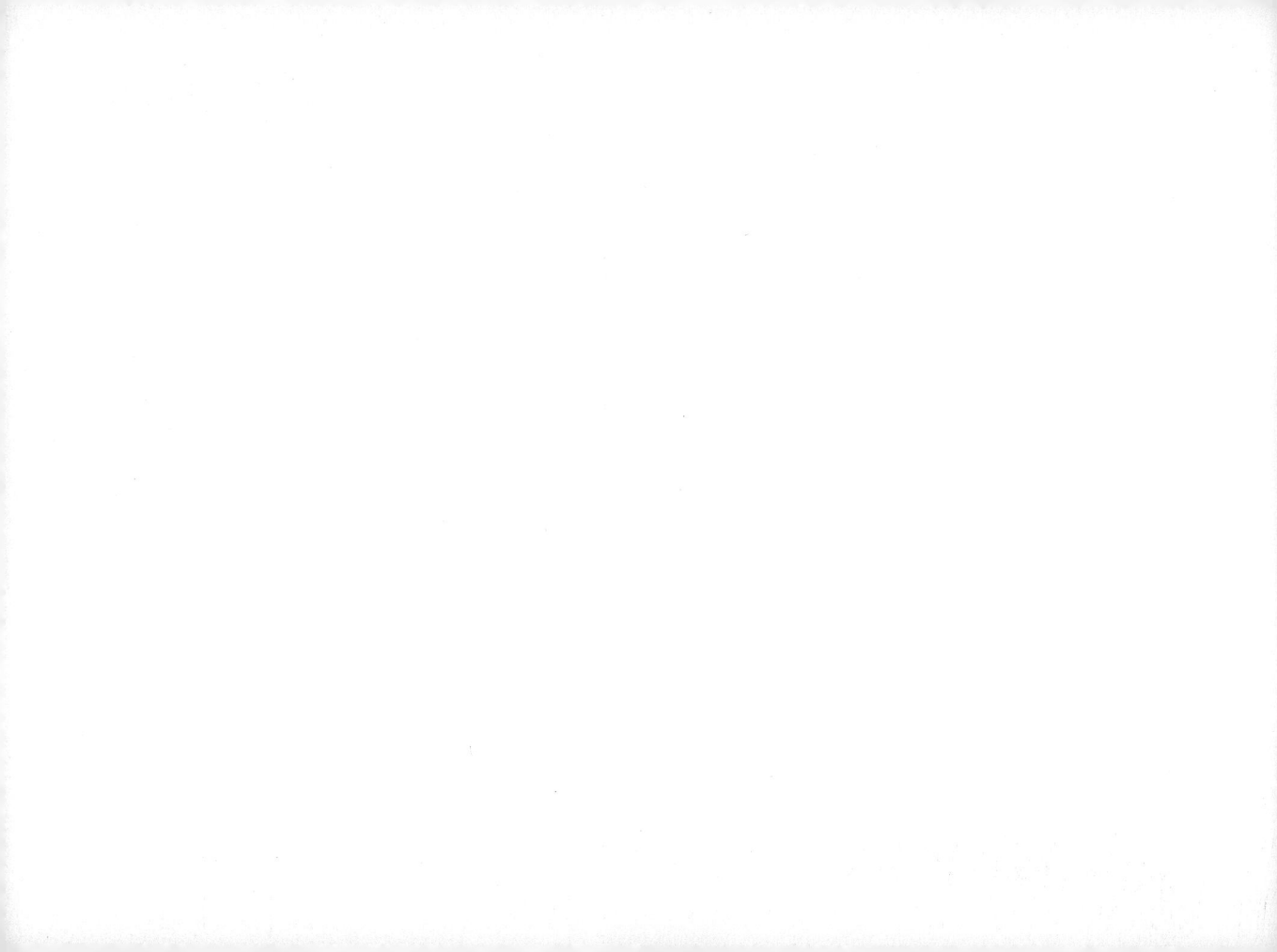

Plates

1. San Diego 1995

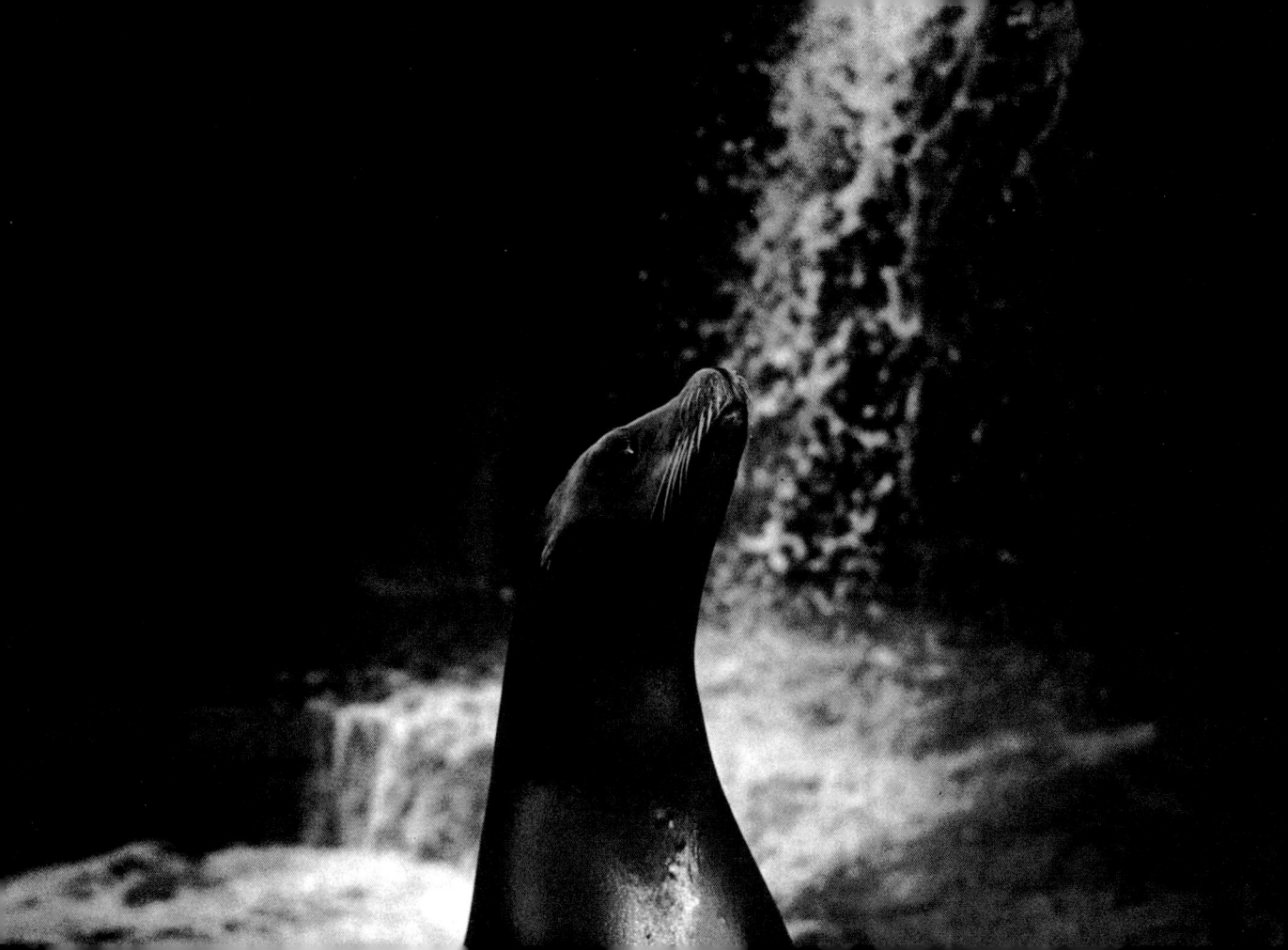

2. London 1992

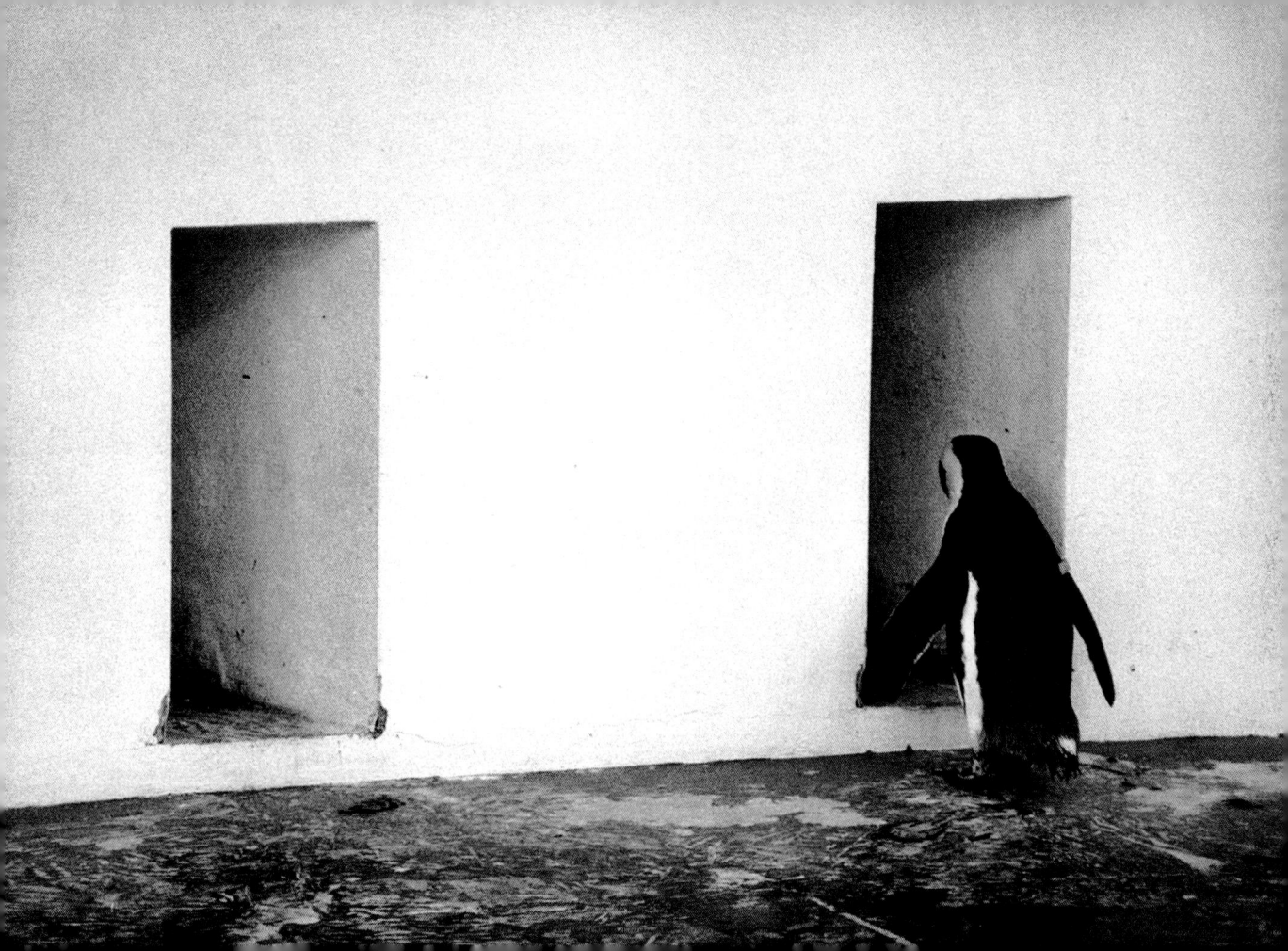

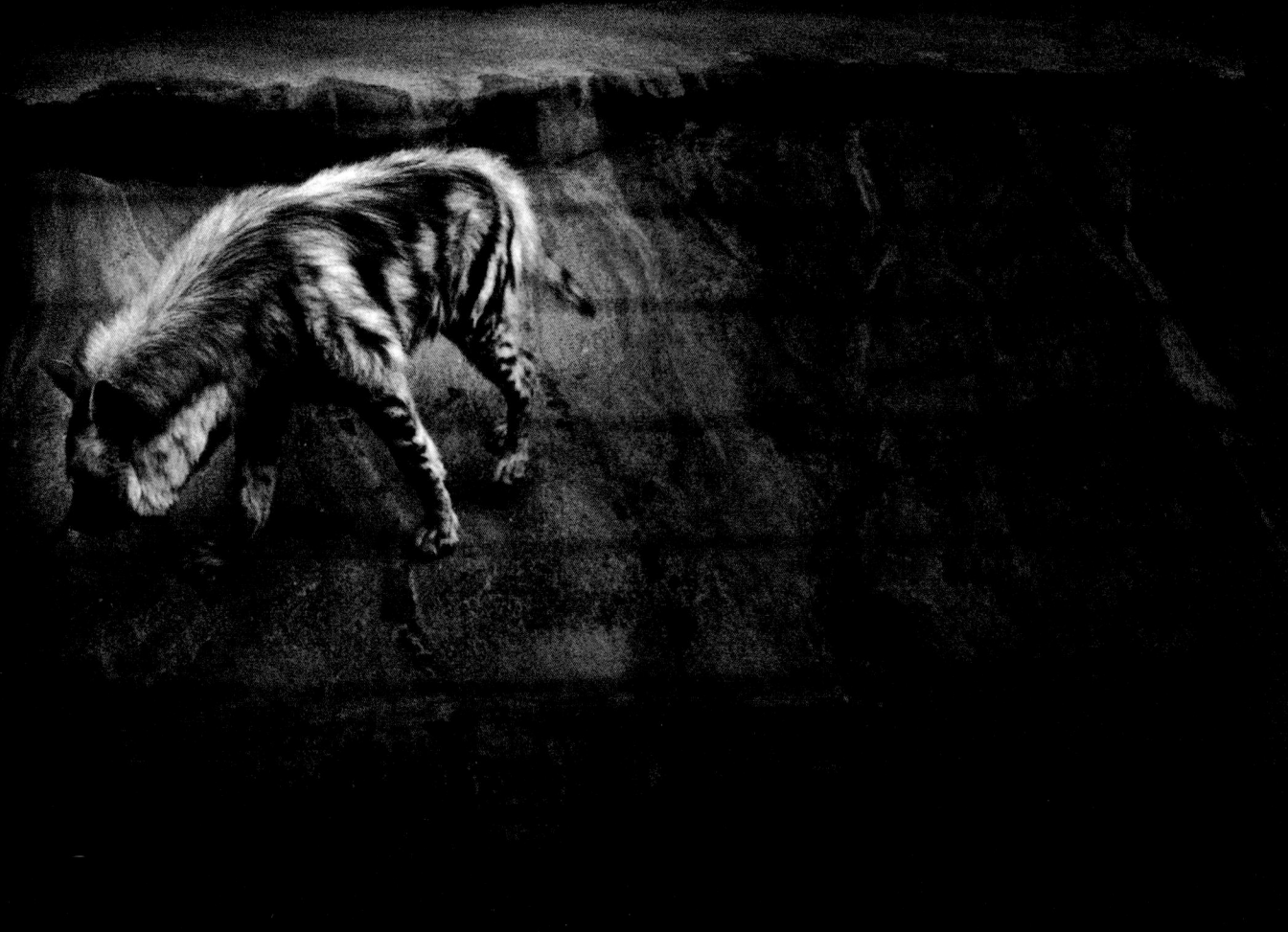

3. San Diego 1995

4. Hanover 1994

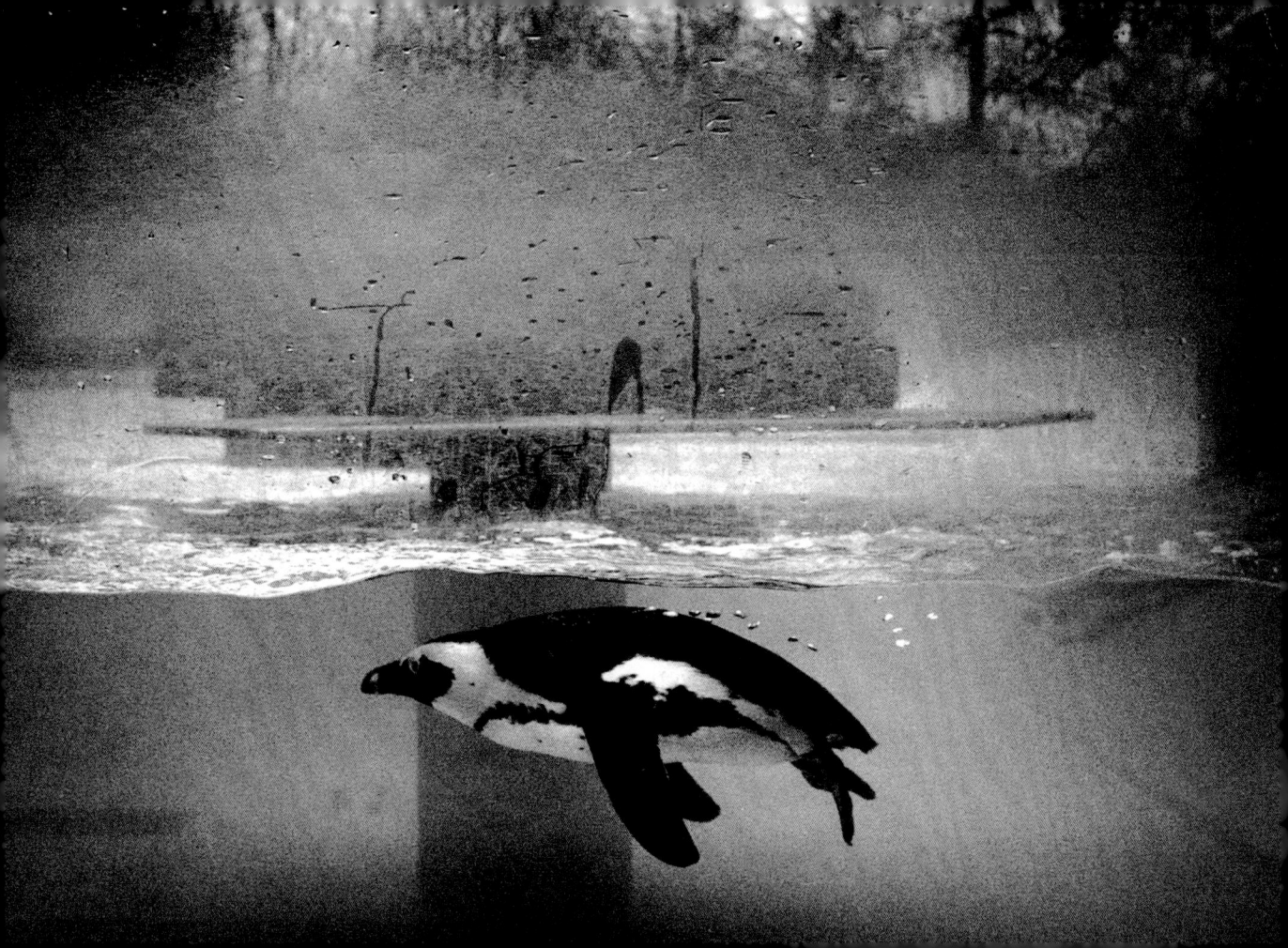

5. Hamburg 1994

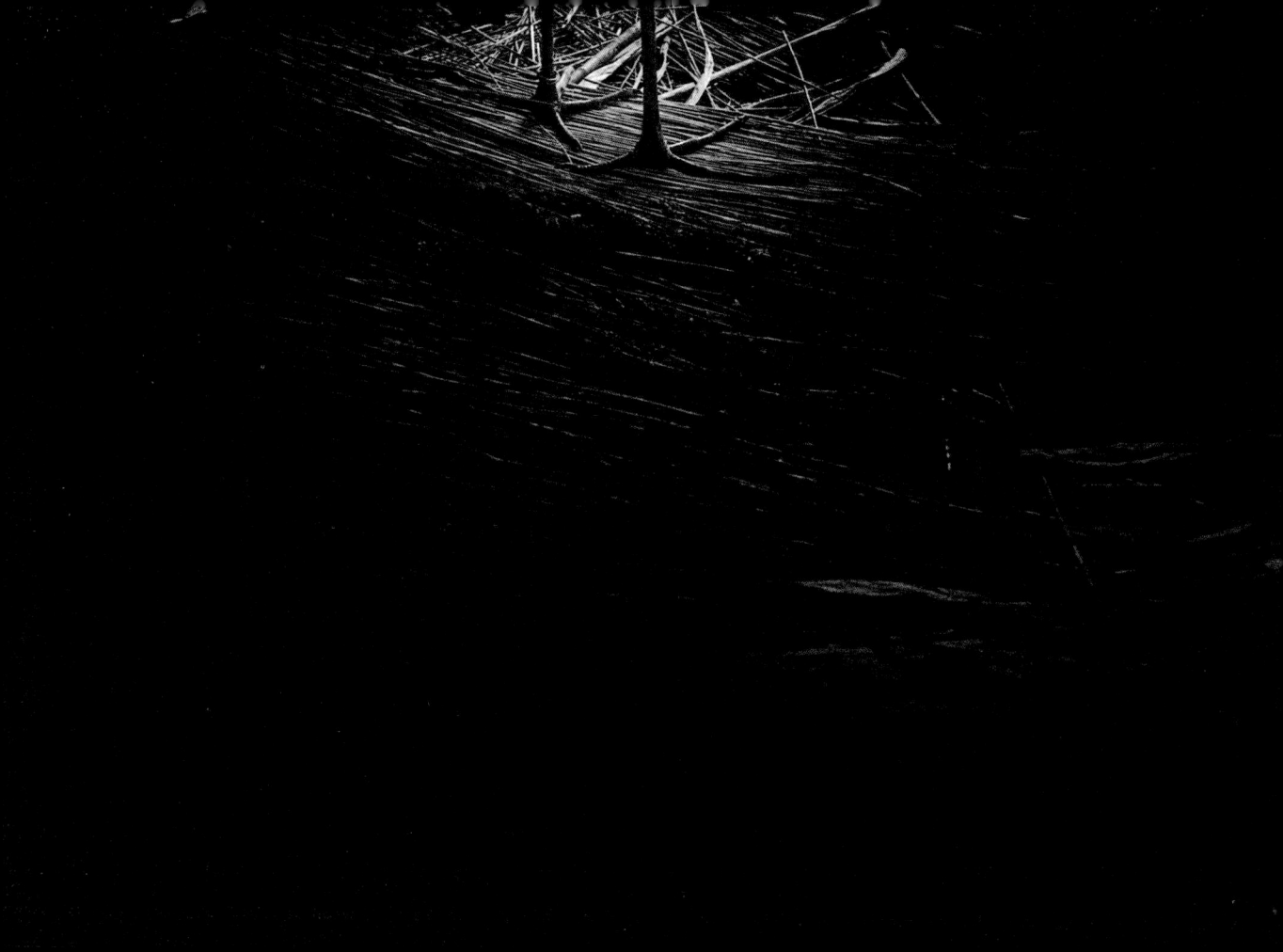

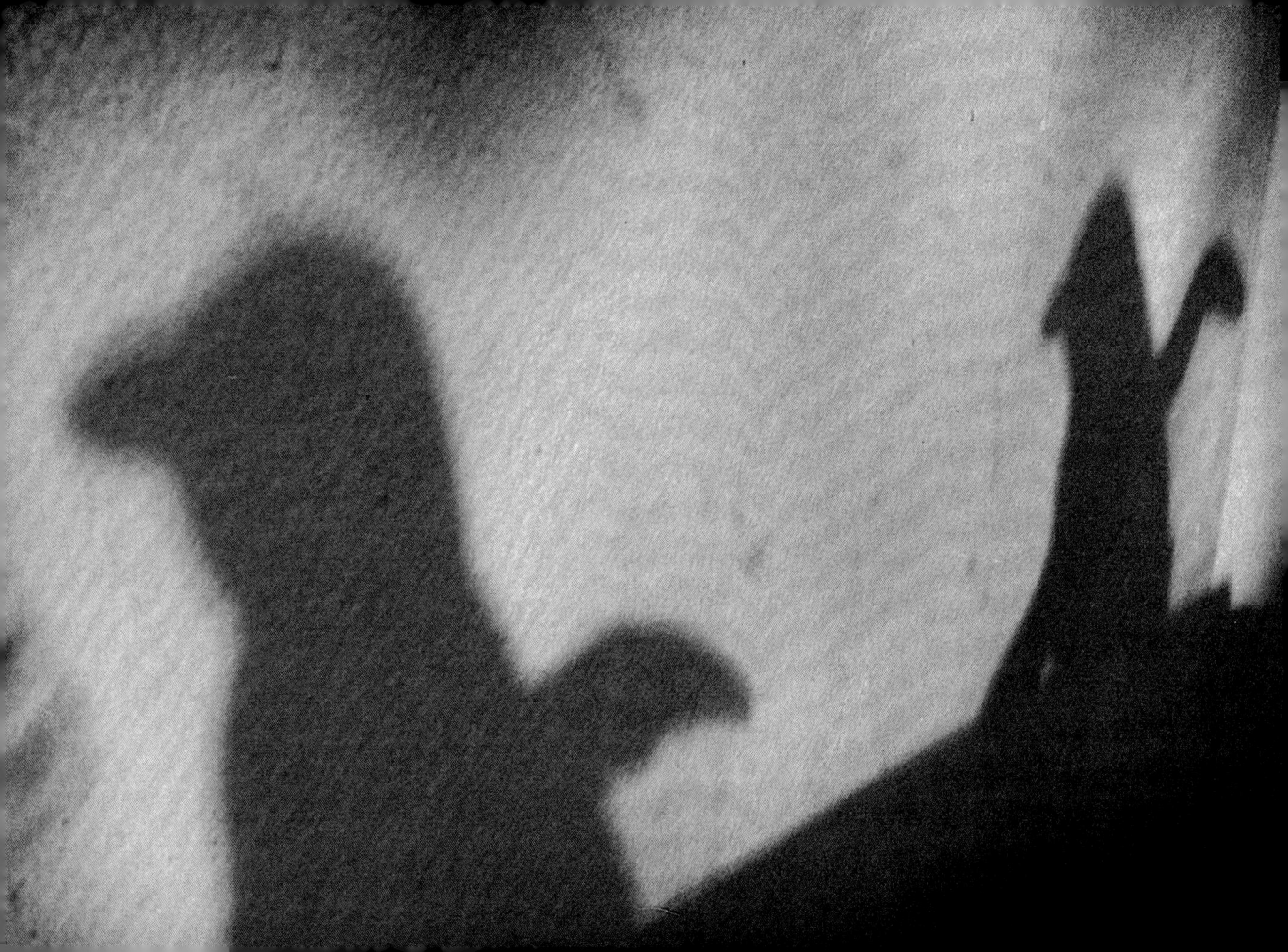

6. London 1995

7. San Diego 1995

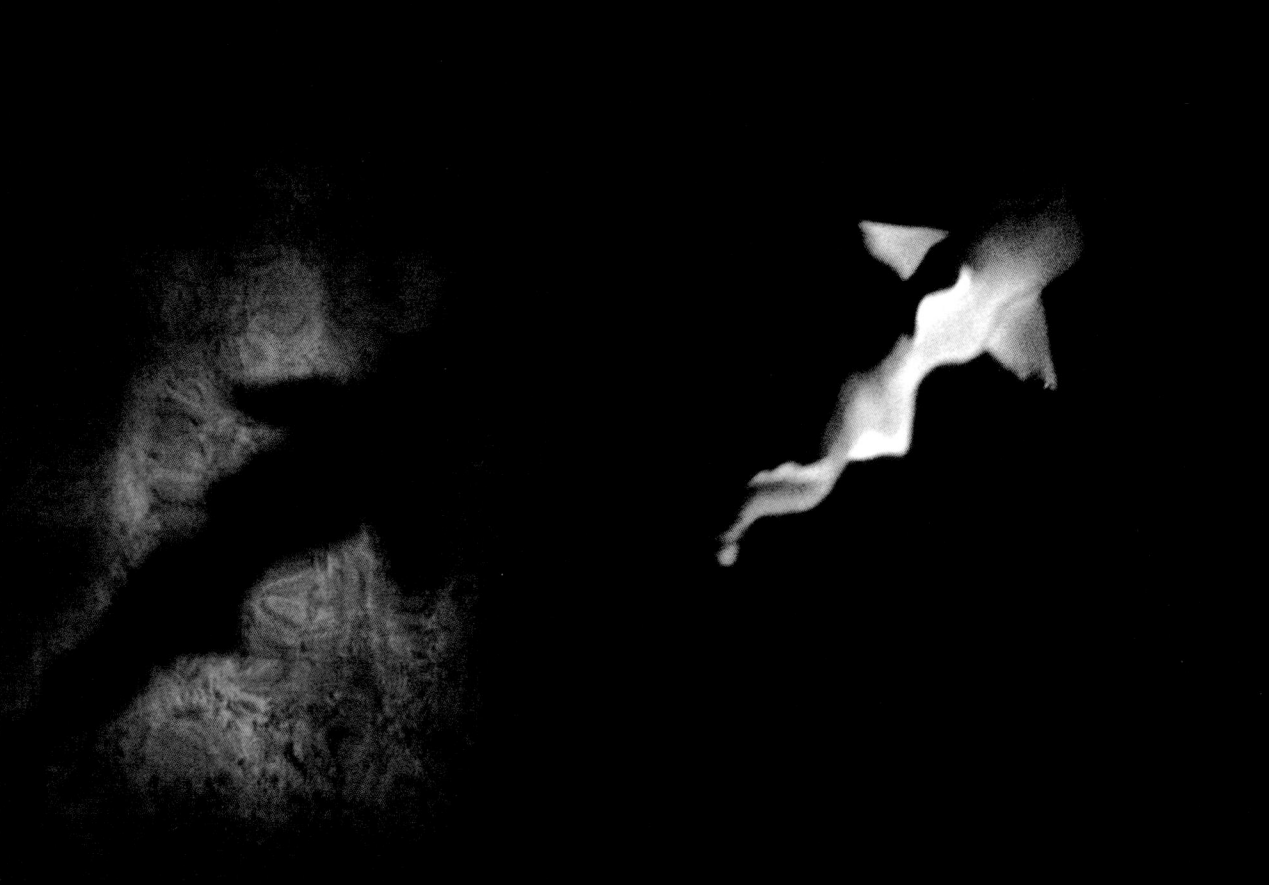

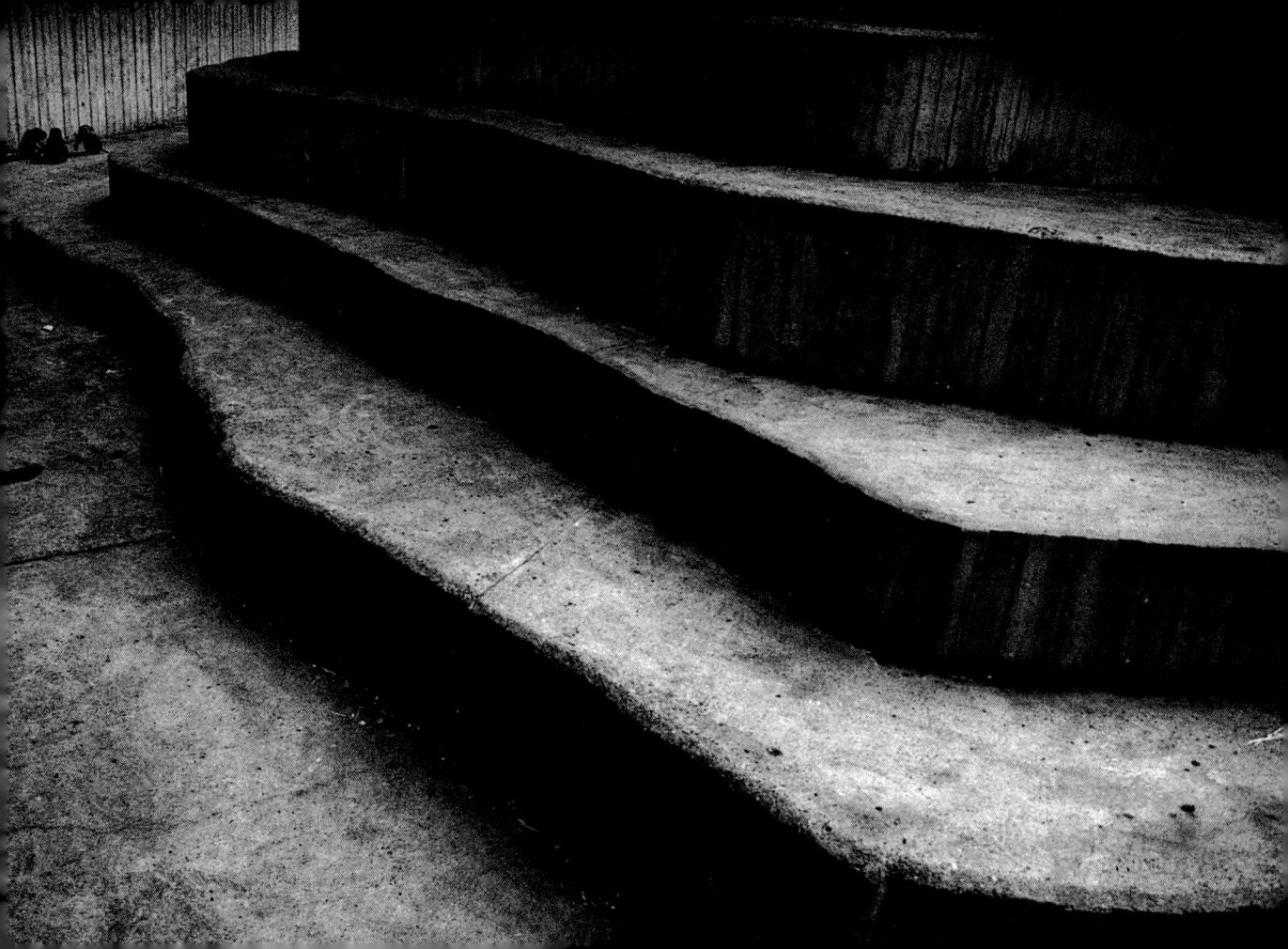

8. Osnabrück 1994

9. London 1992

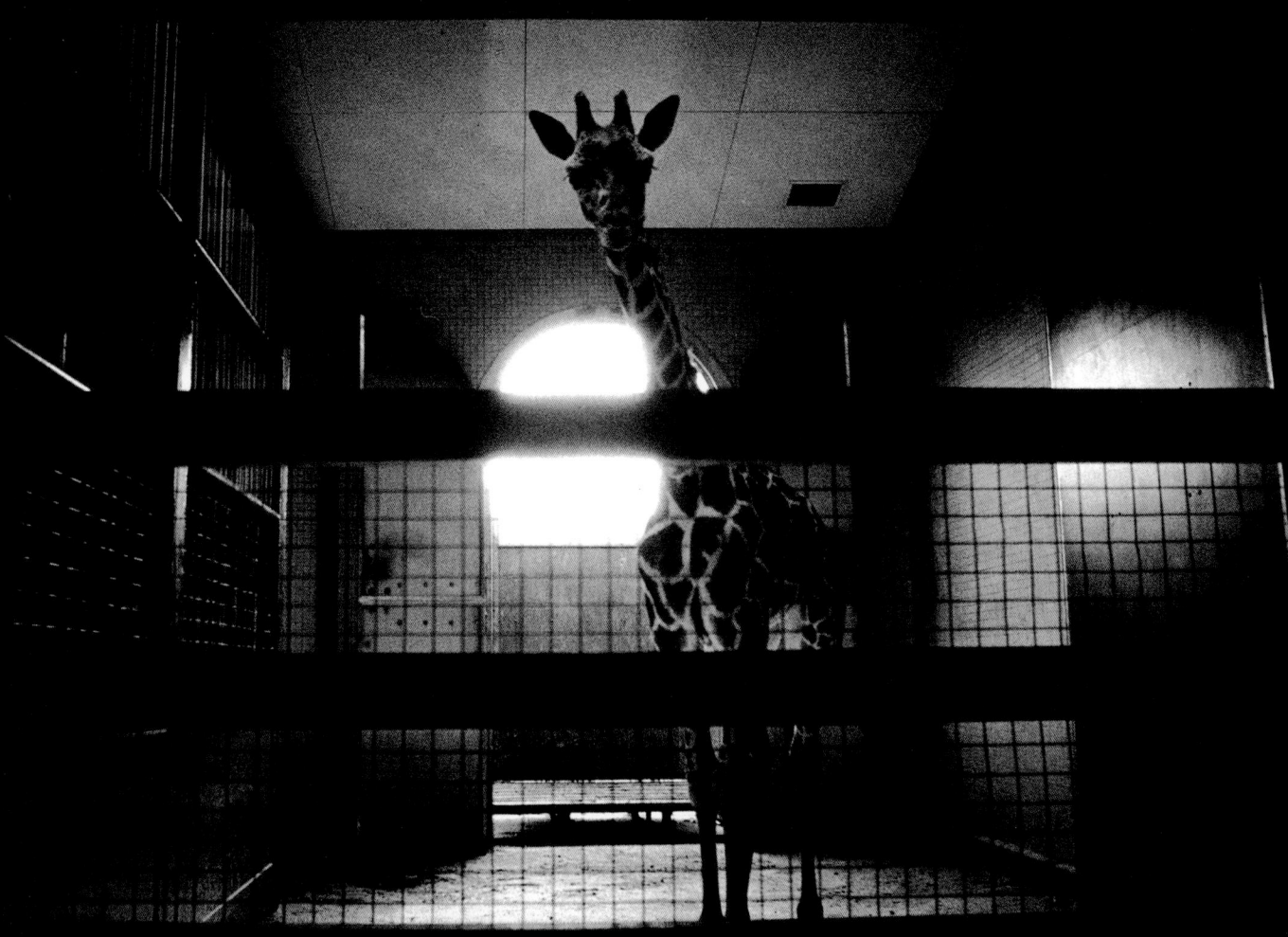

10. Palm Springs 1995

11. Berlin 1992

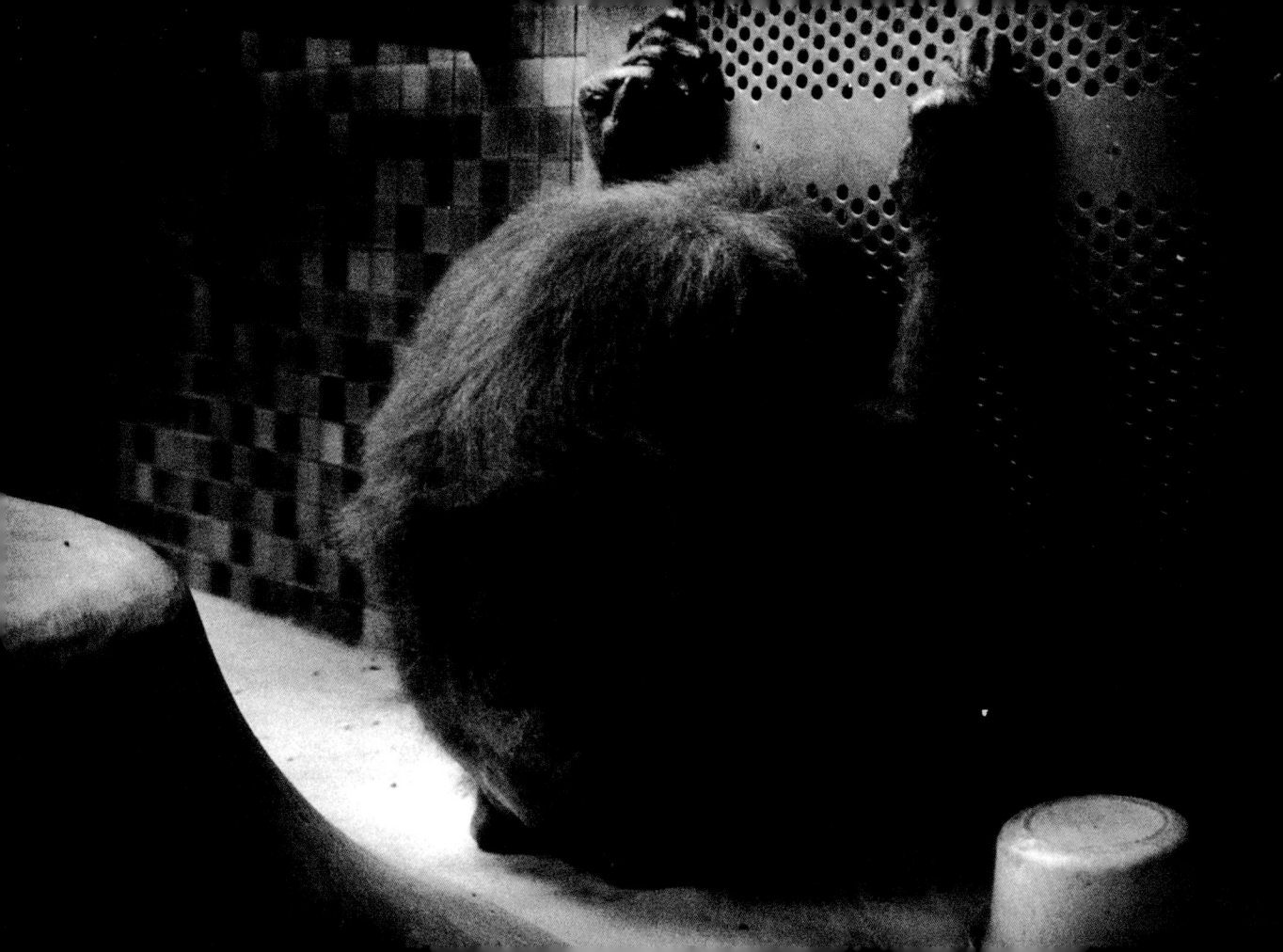

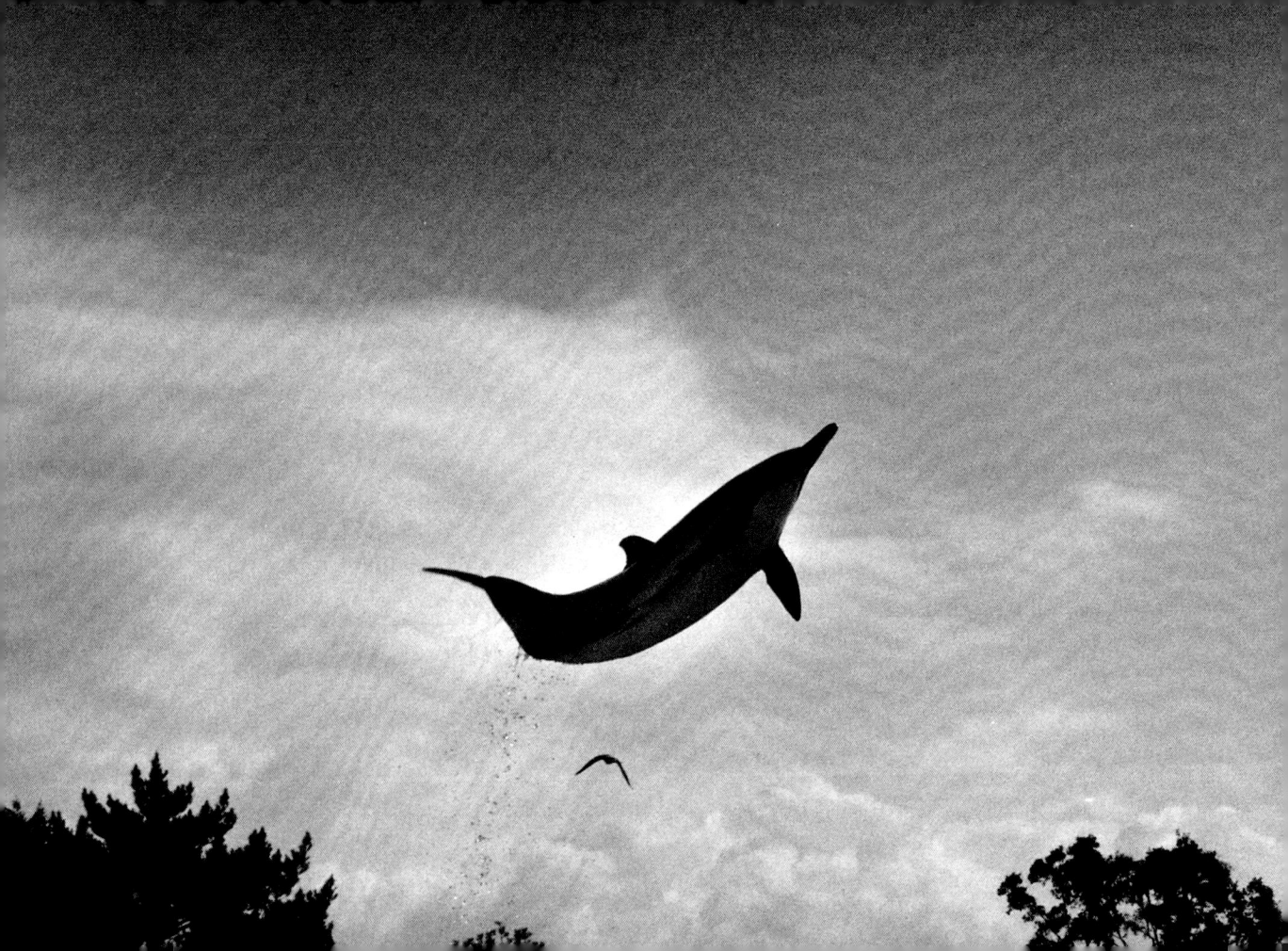

12. San Diego 1995

13. Berlin 1992

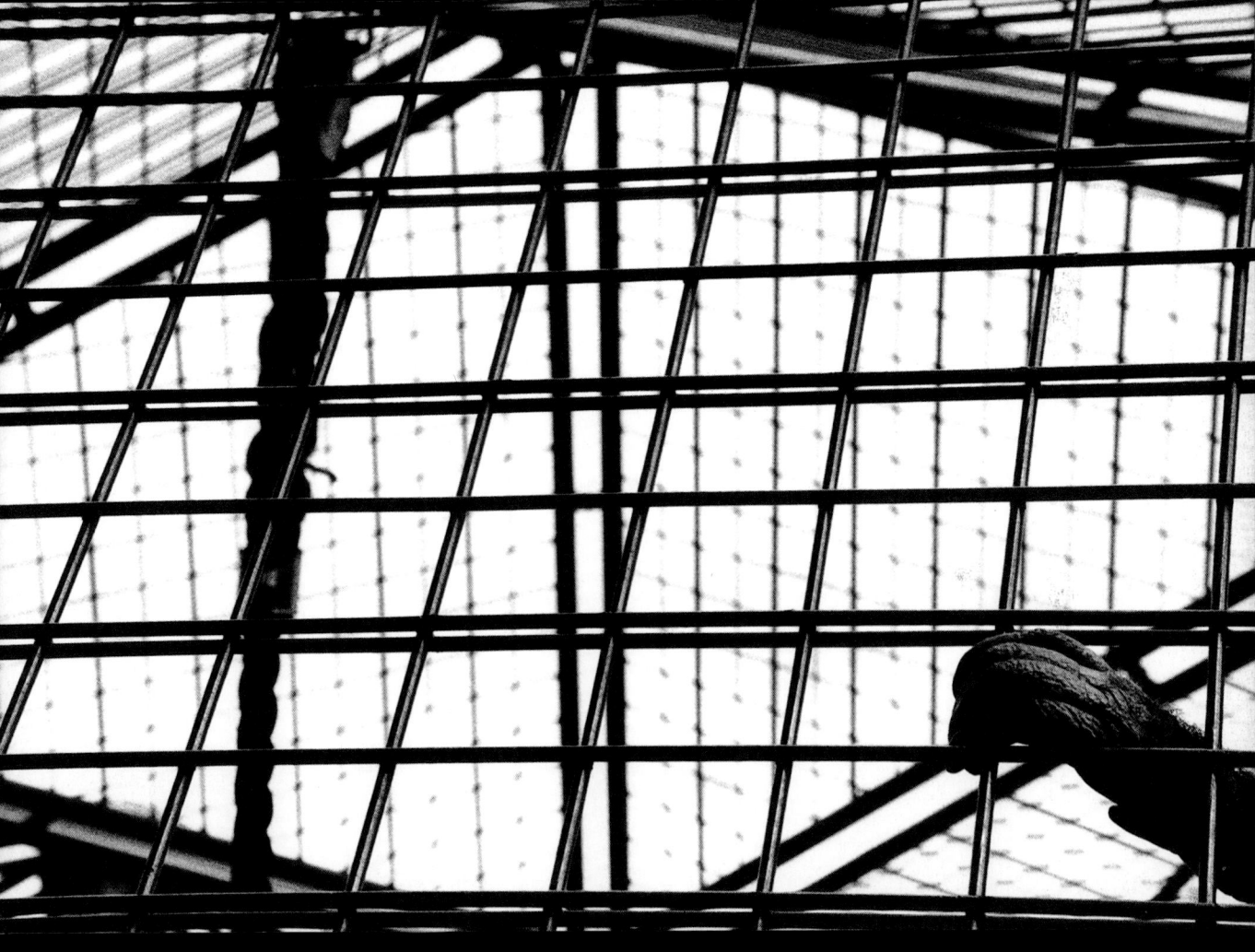

14. Hamburg 1994

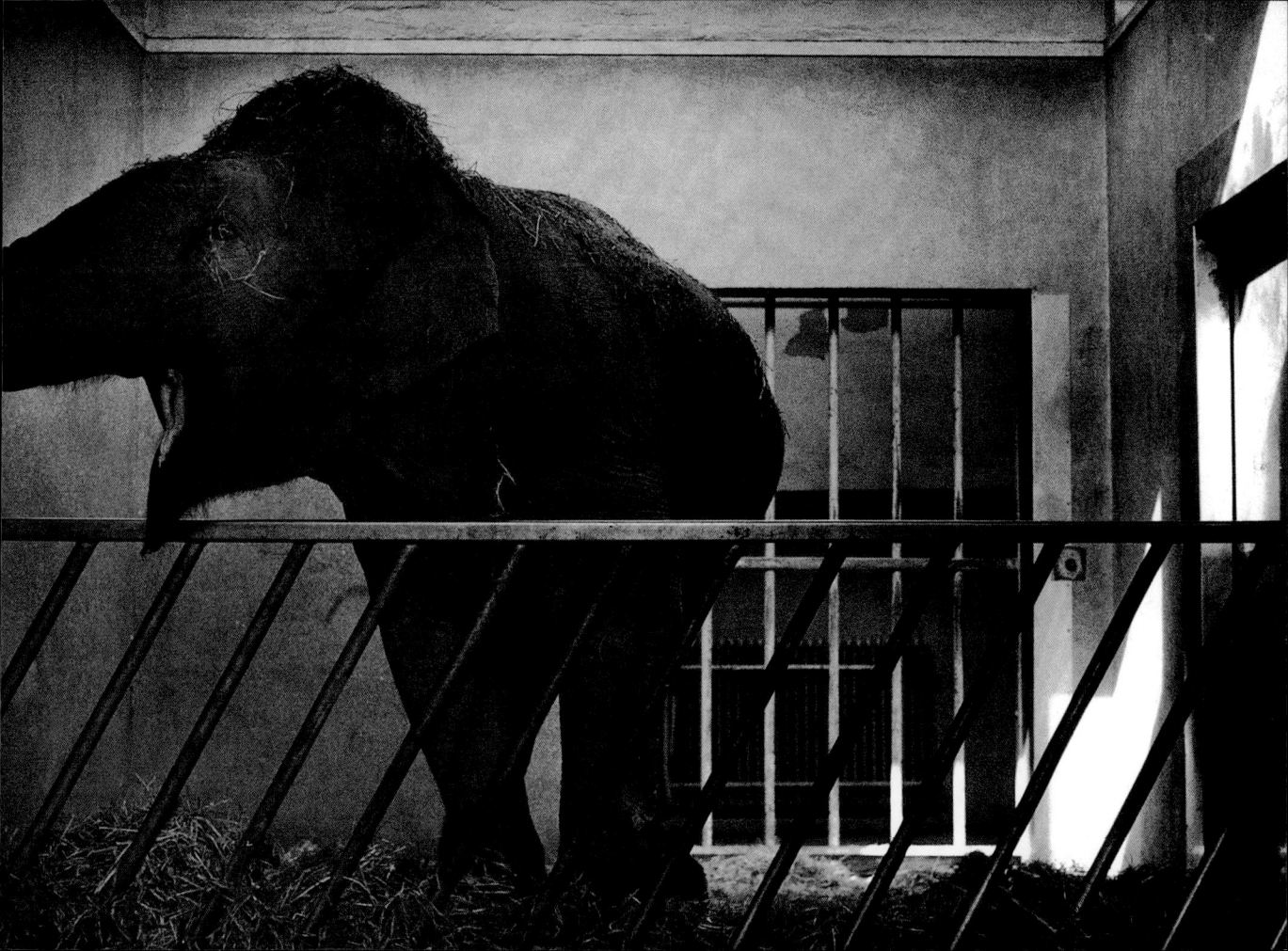

15. Bremerhaven 1993

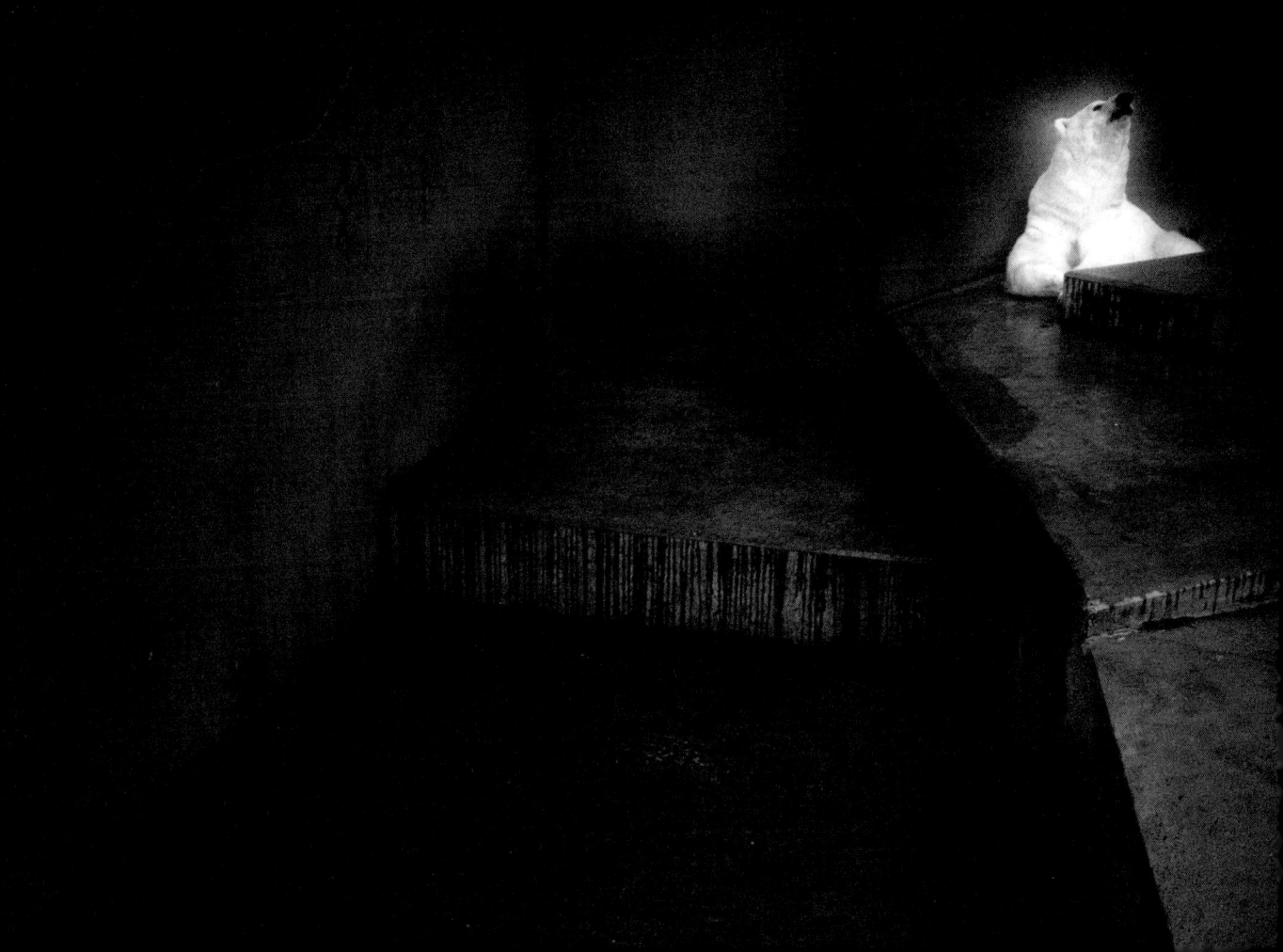

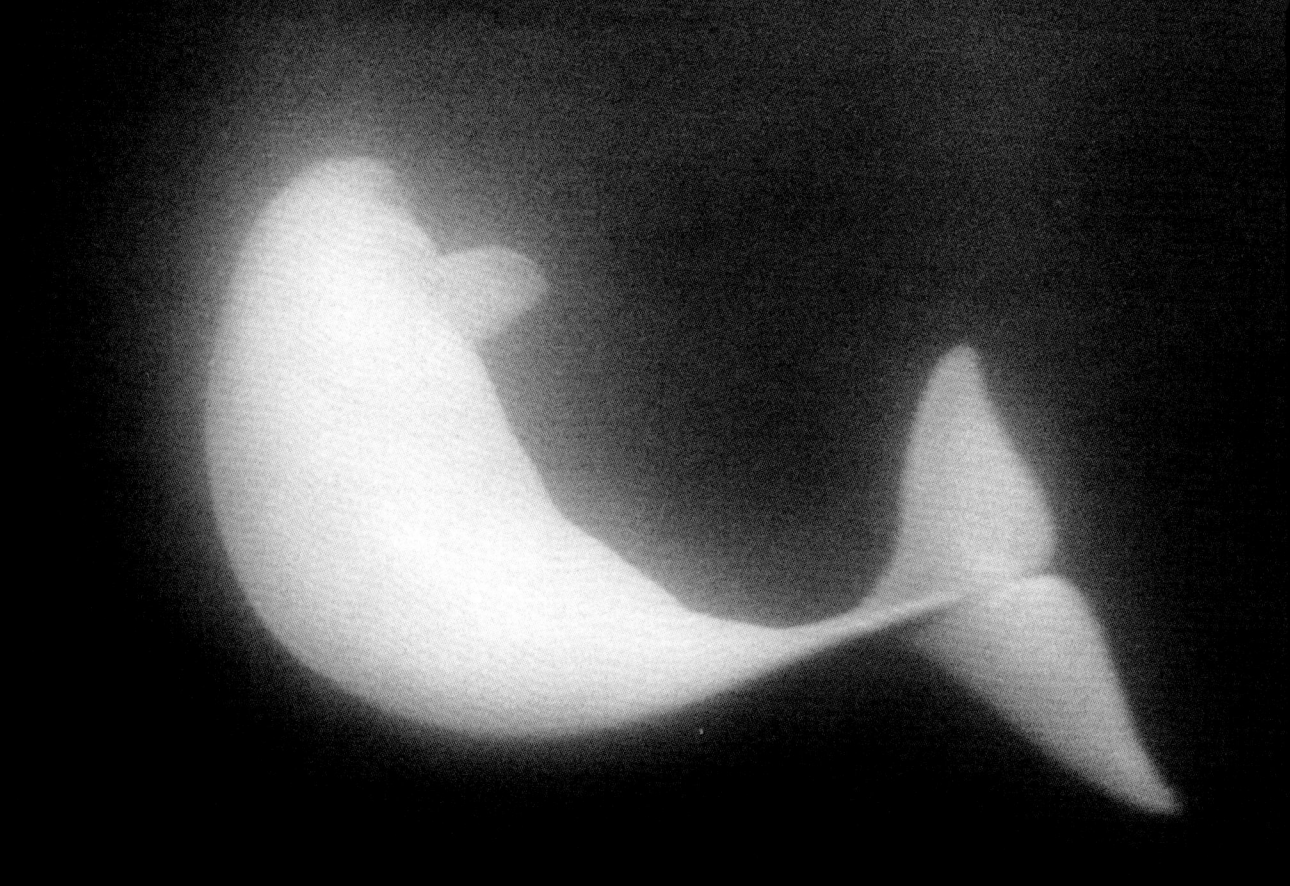

16. New York 1995

17. Dublin 1992

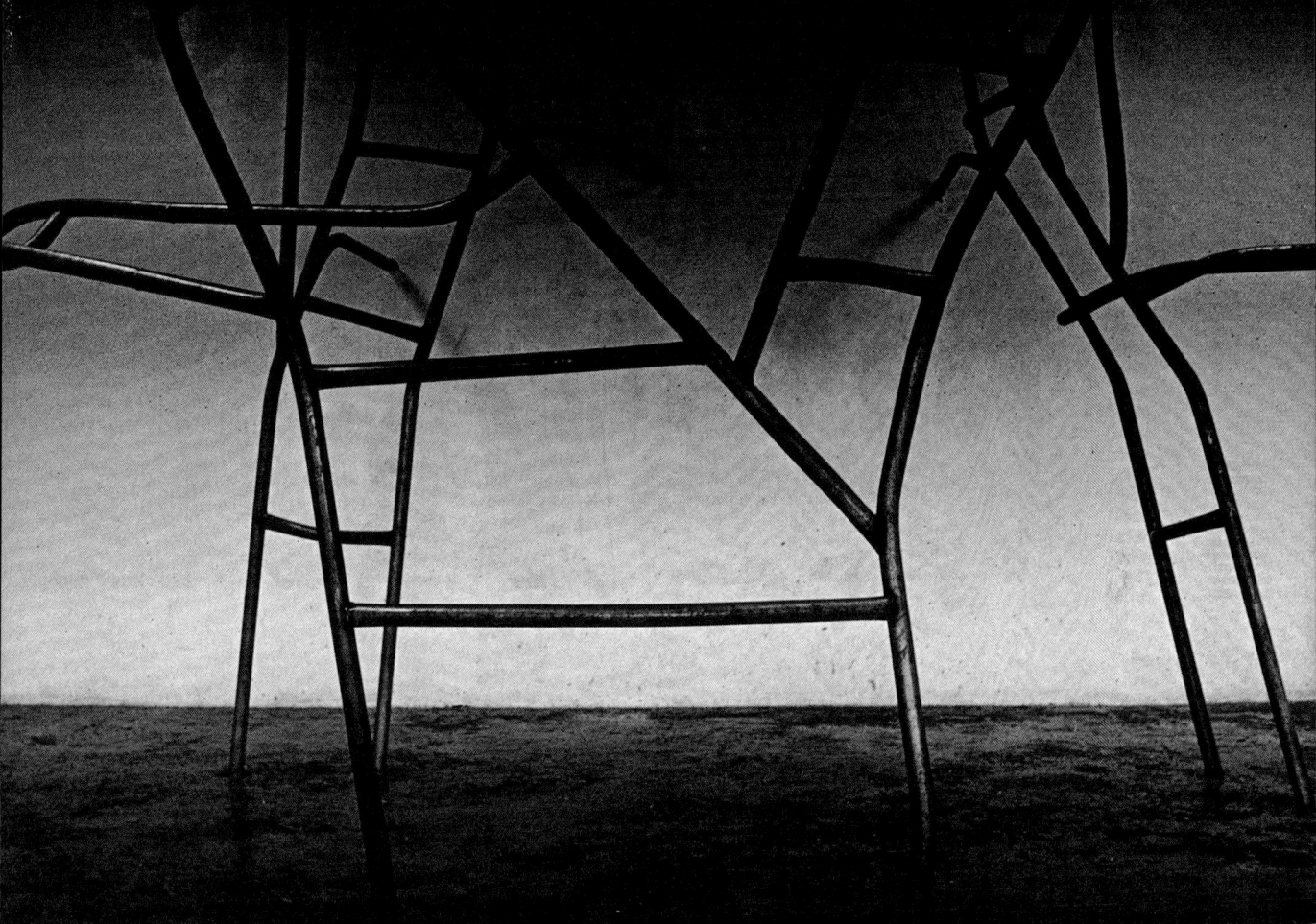

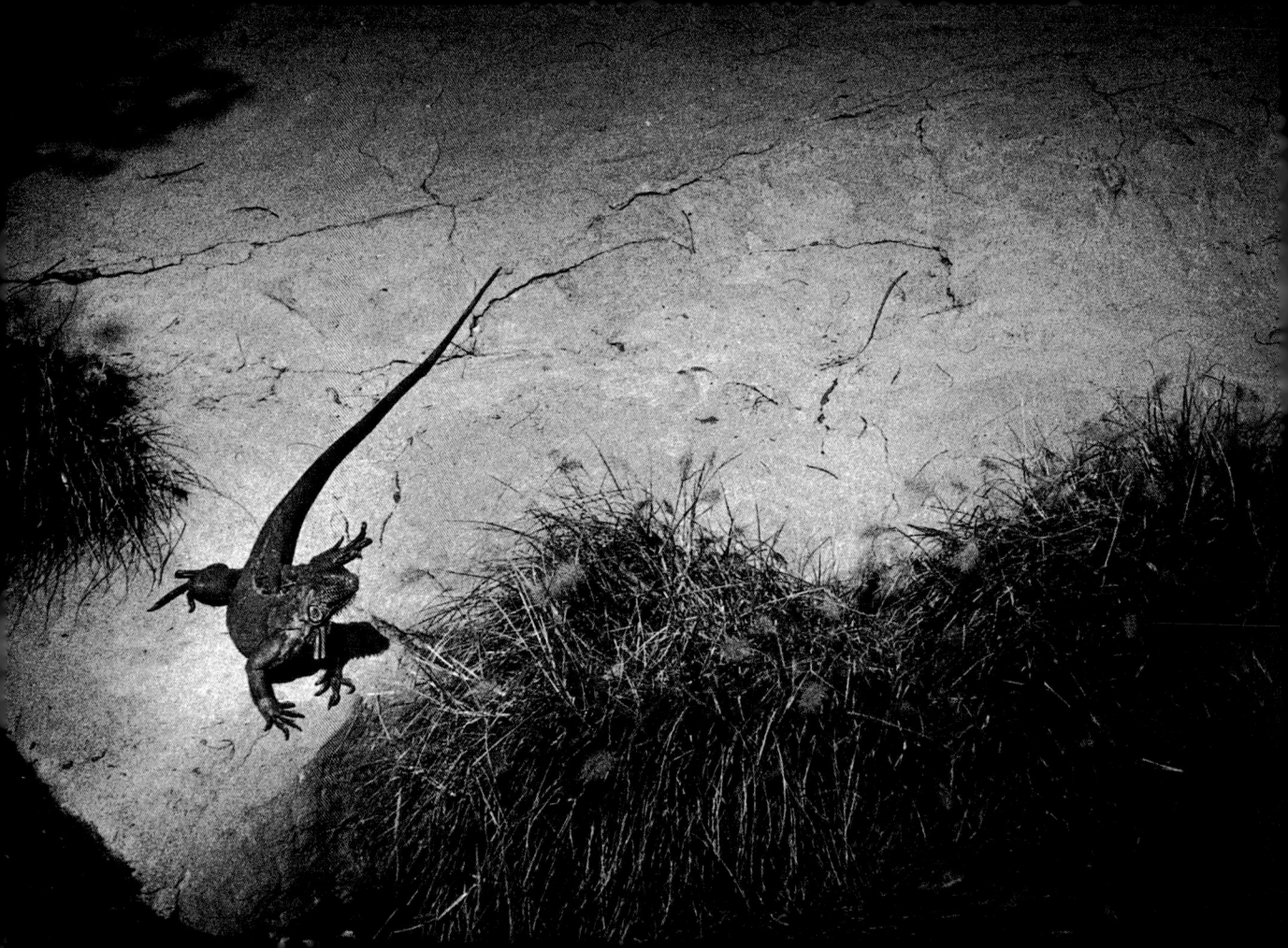

18. San Diego 1995

19. San Diego 1995

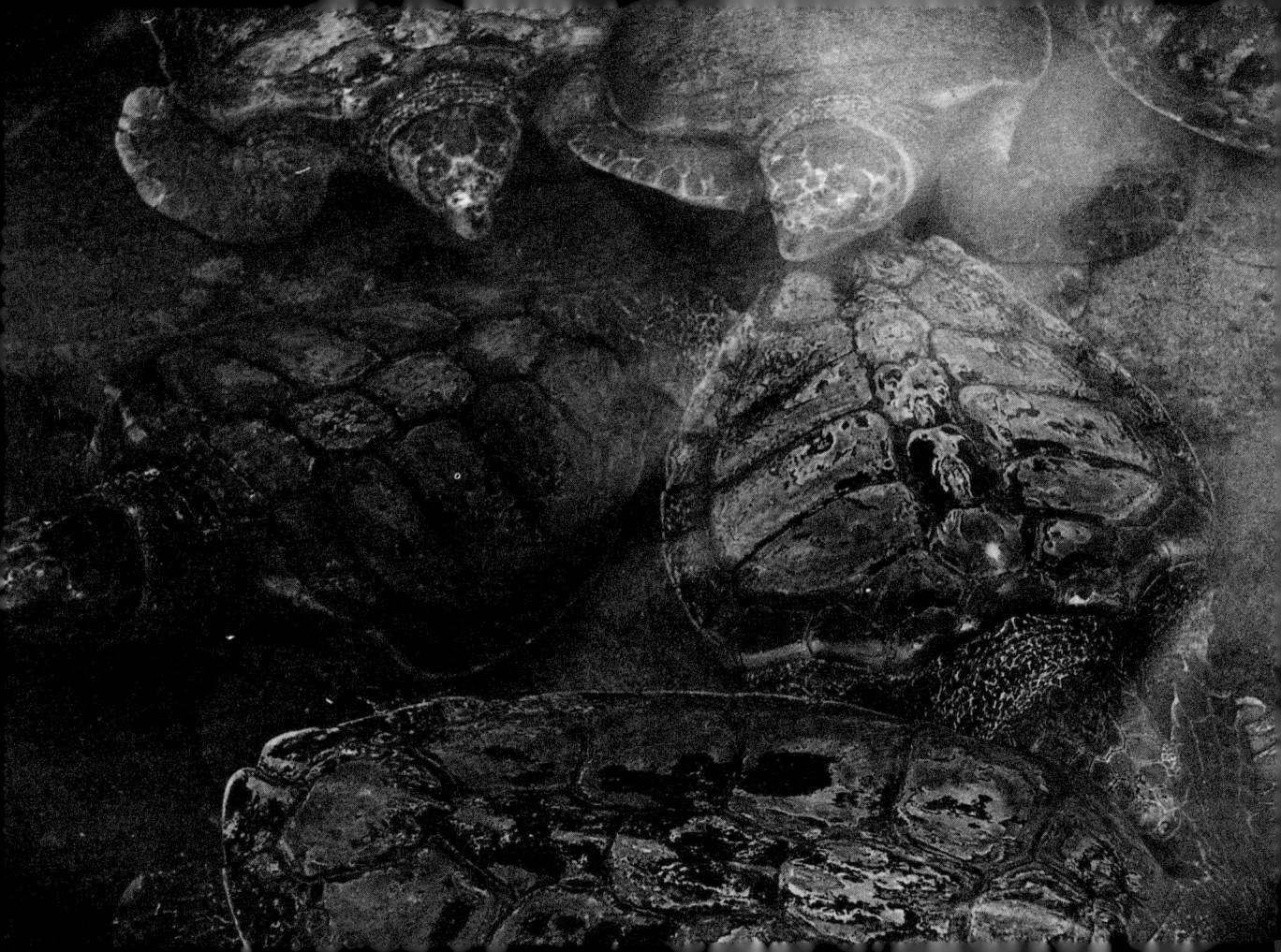

20. New York 1995

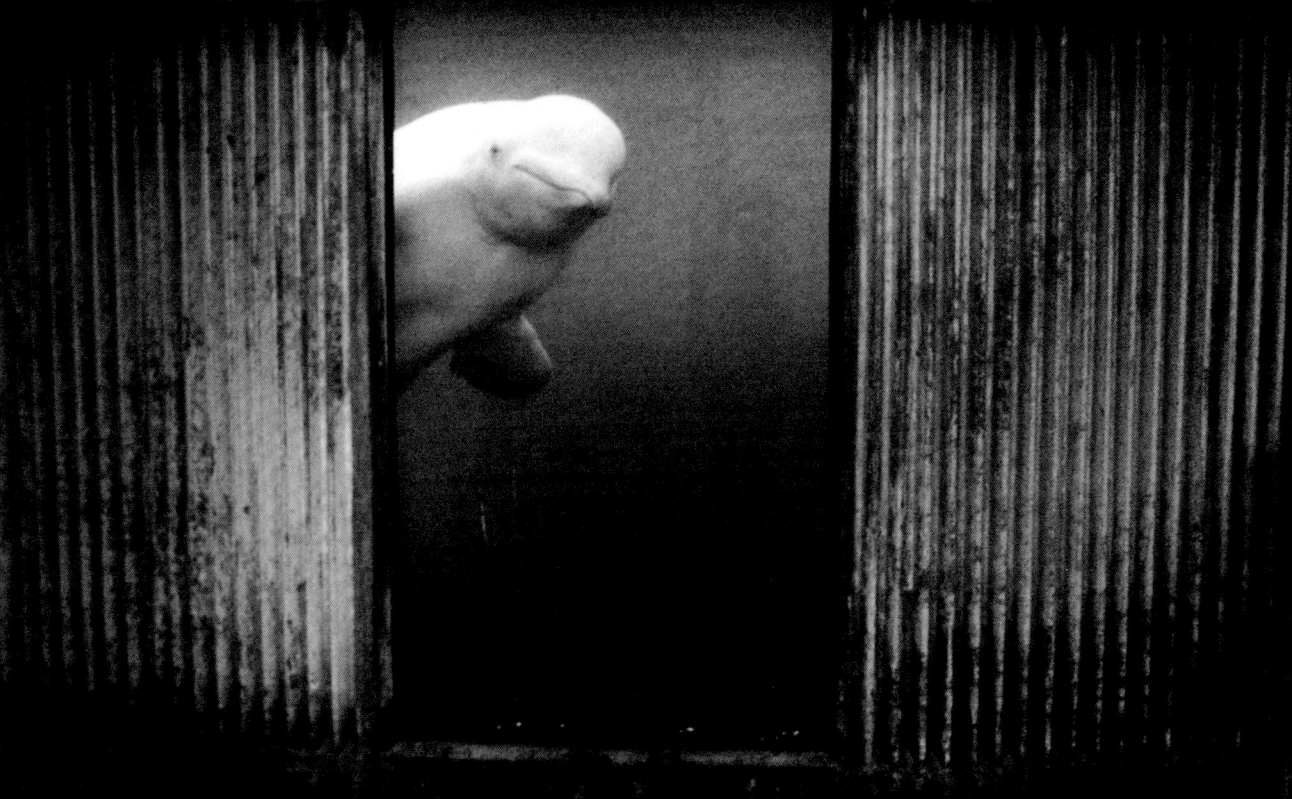

21. London 1992

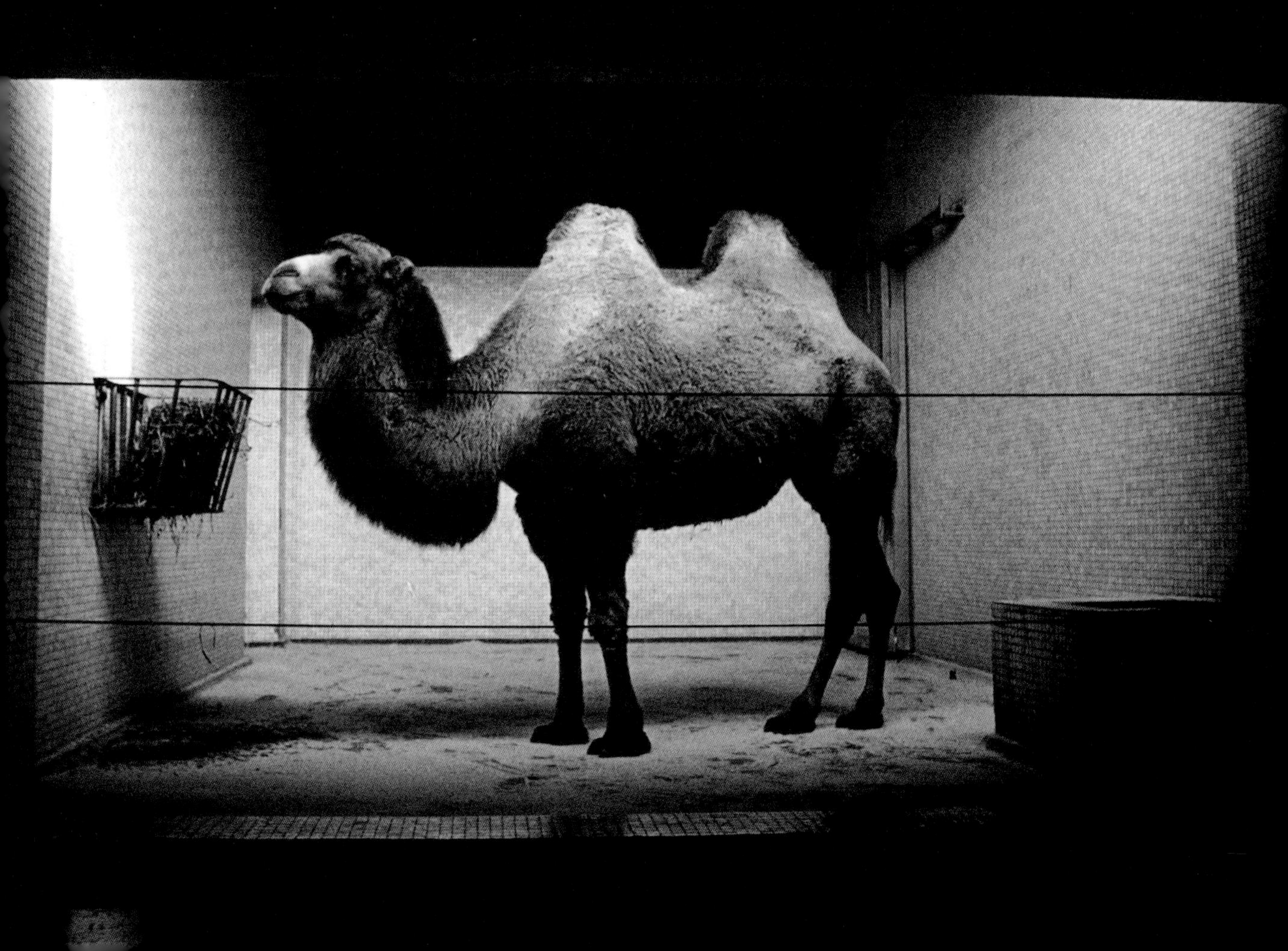

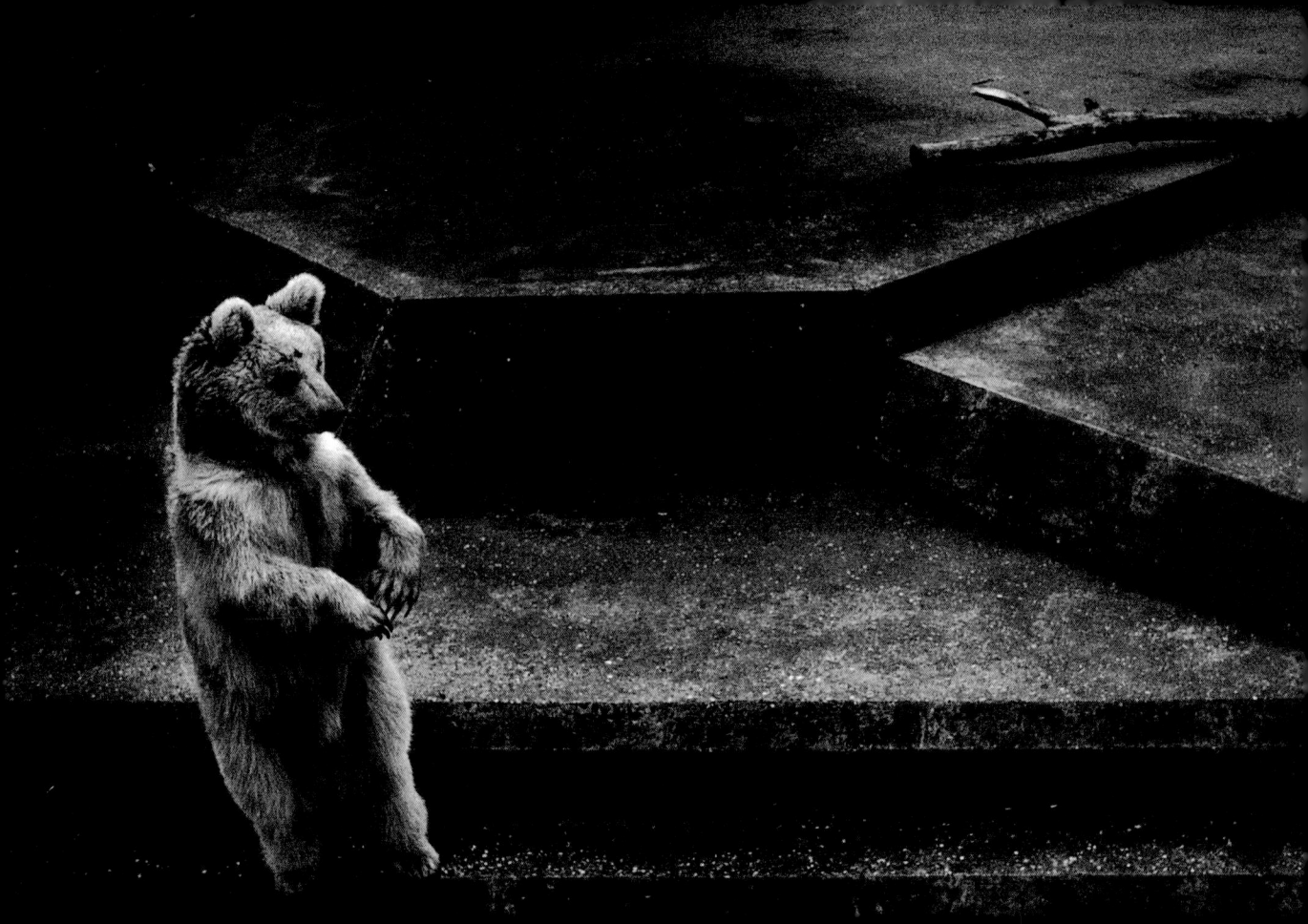

22. Münster 1994

23. San Diego 1995

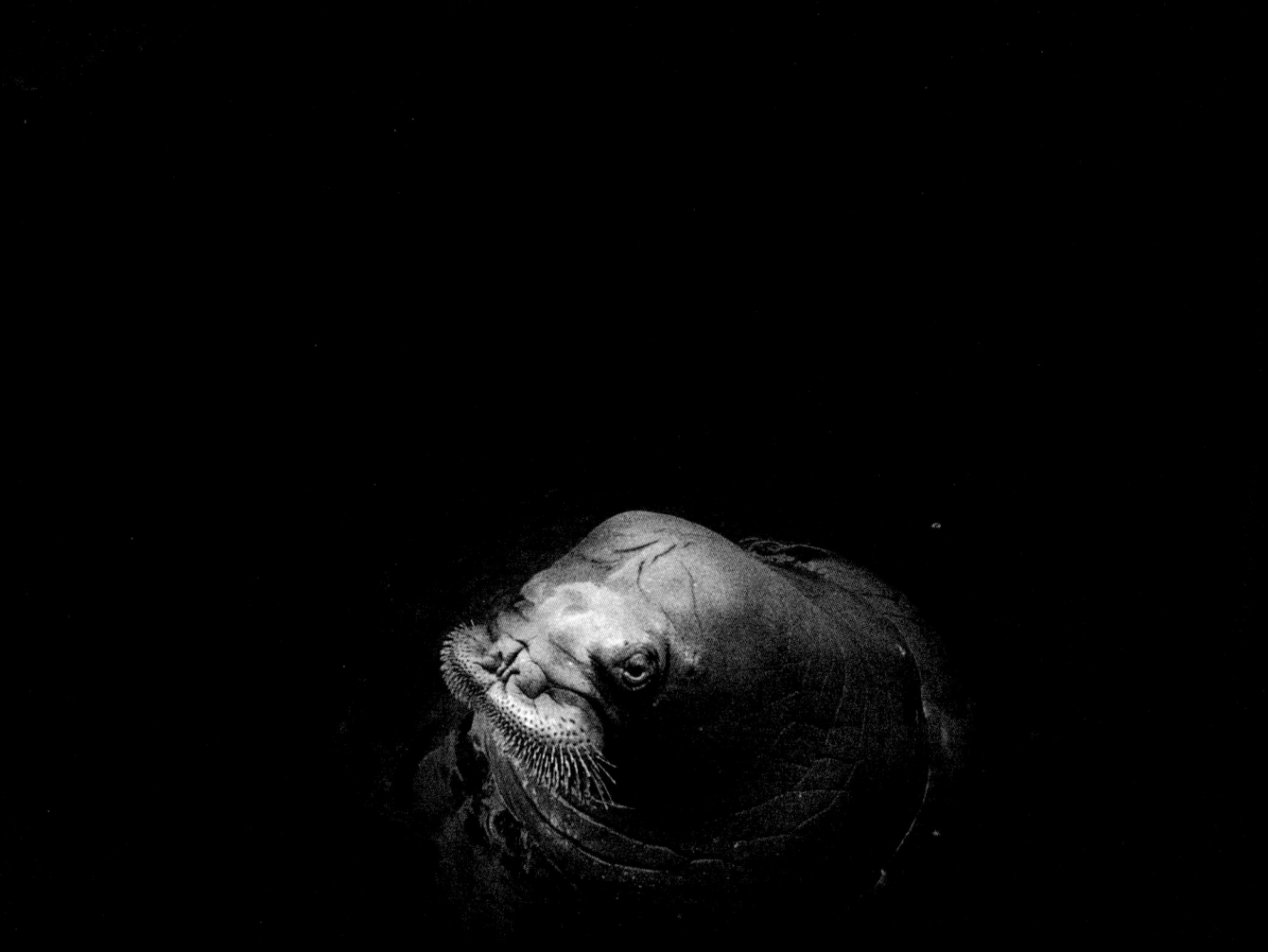

24. London 1992

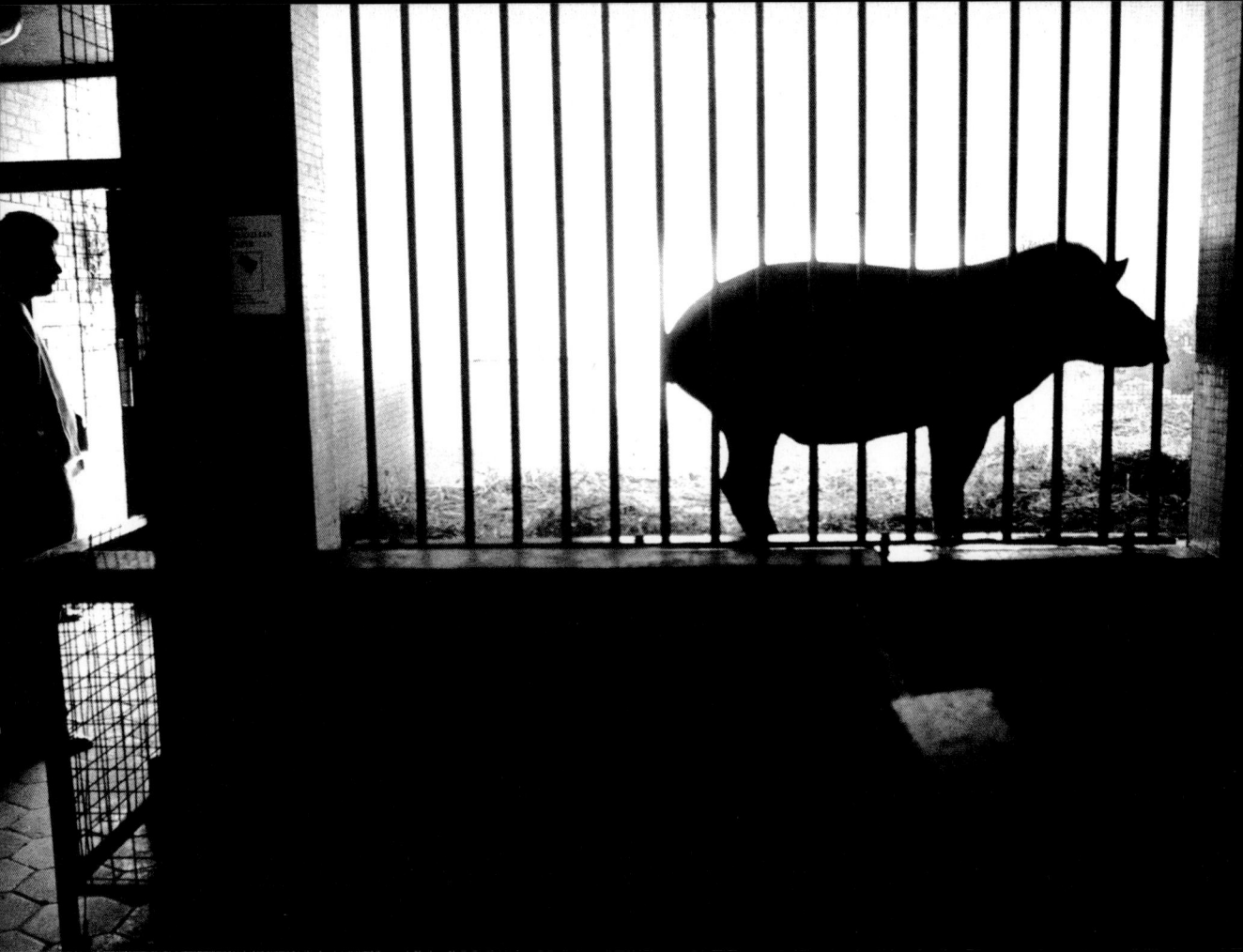

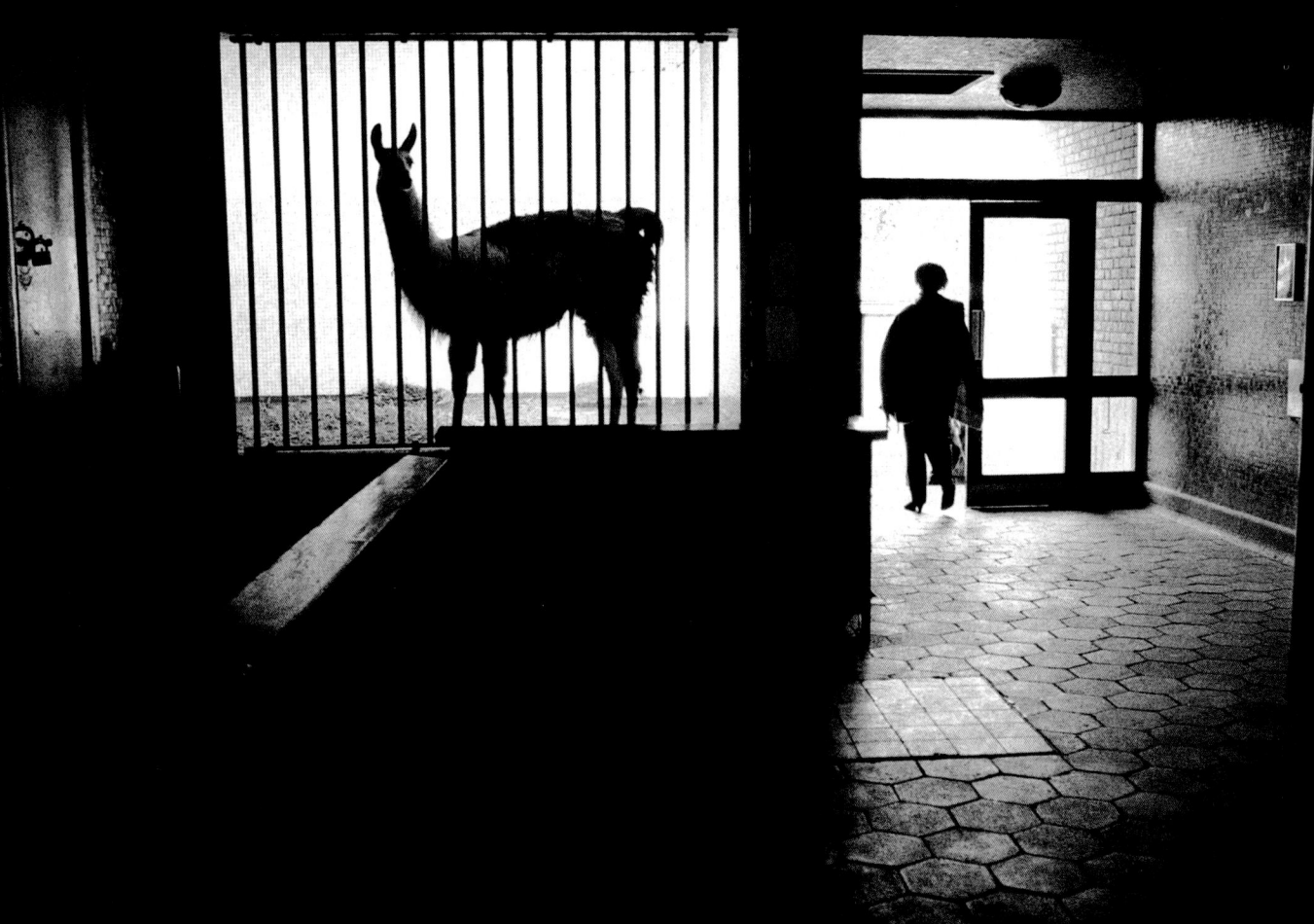

25. London 1992

26. Bremerhaven 1994

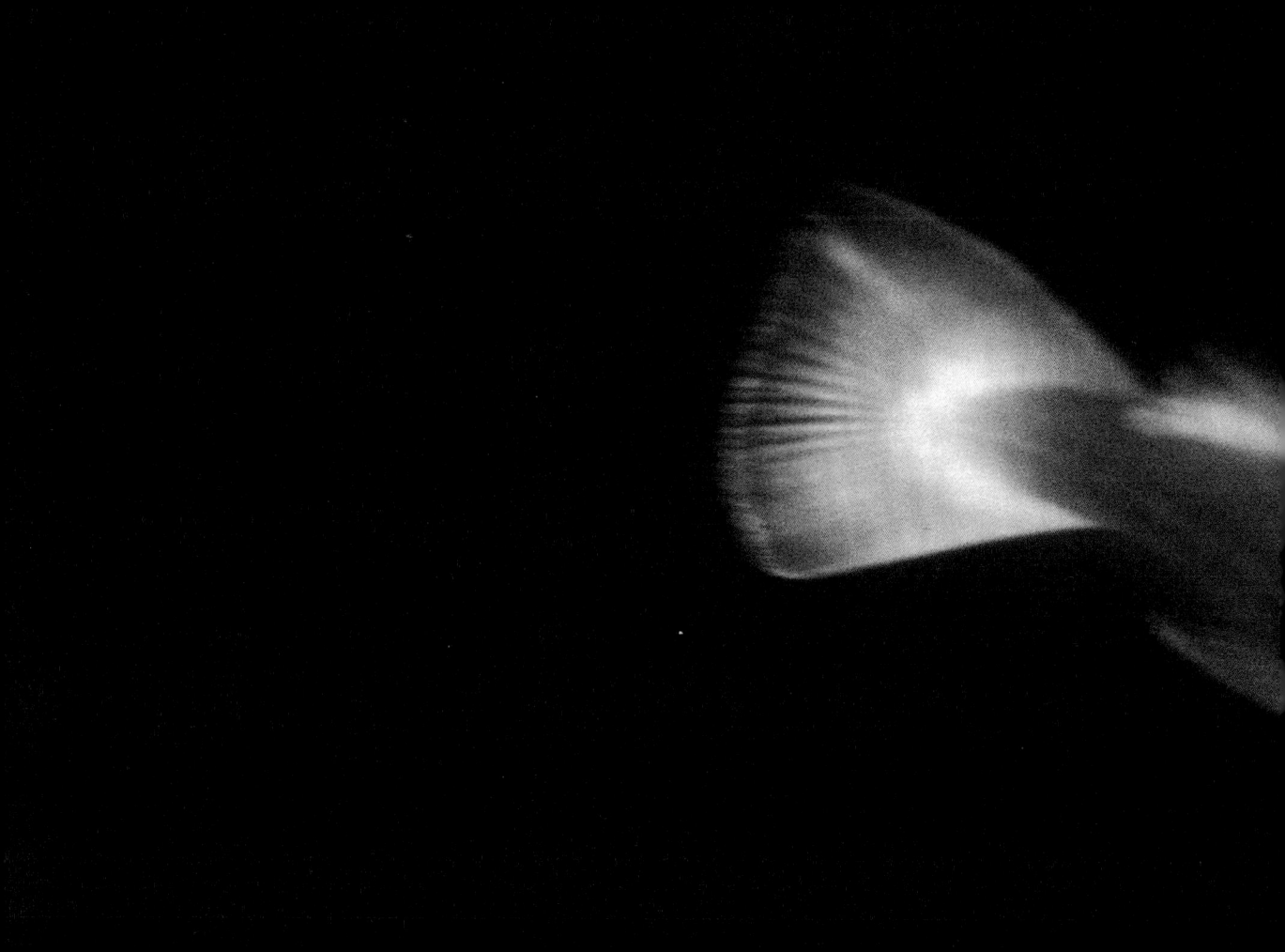

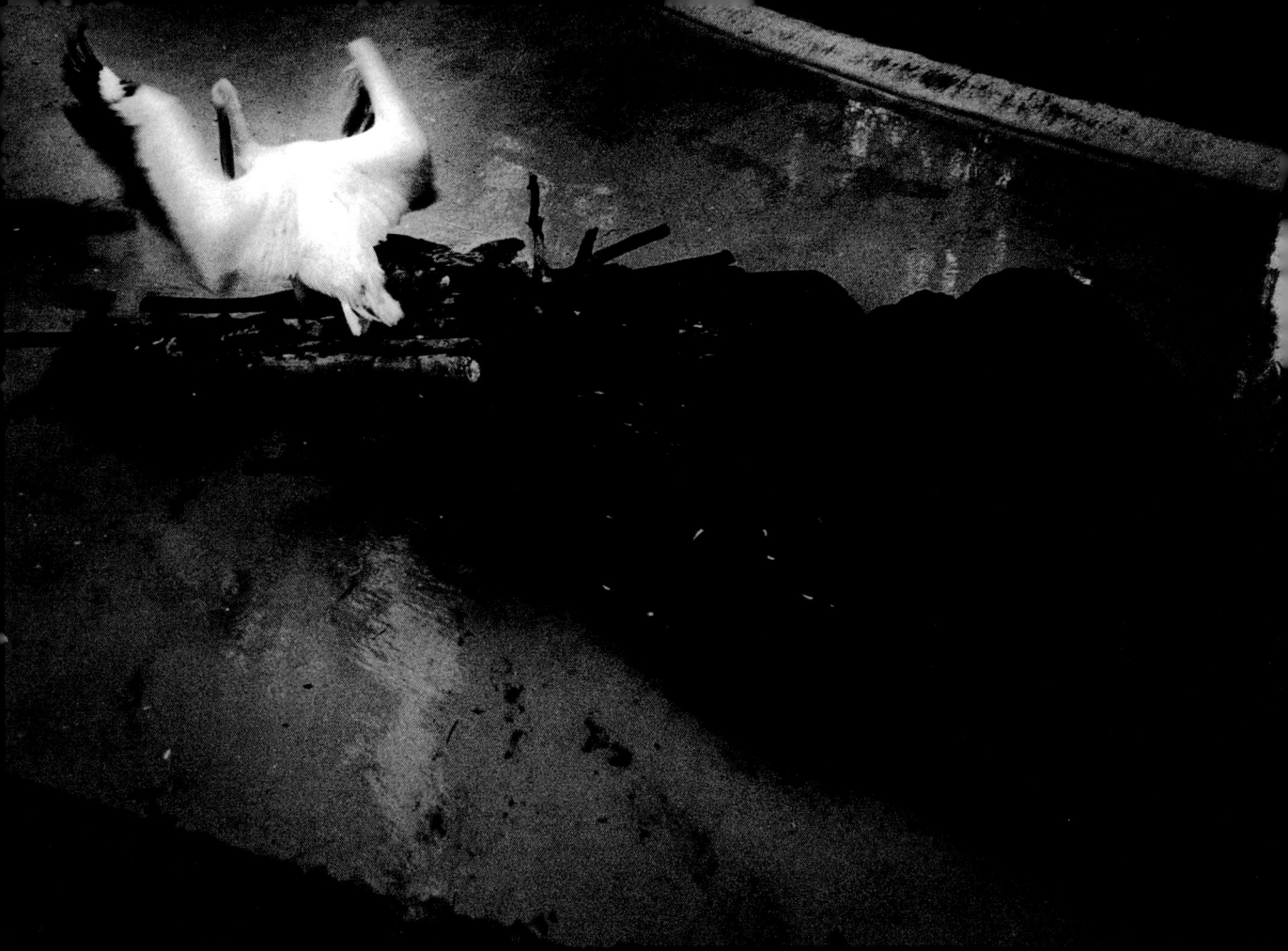

27. Los Angeles 1995

28. Chessington 1994

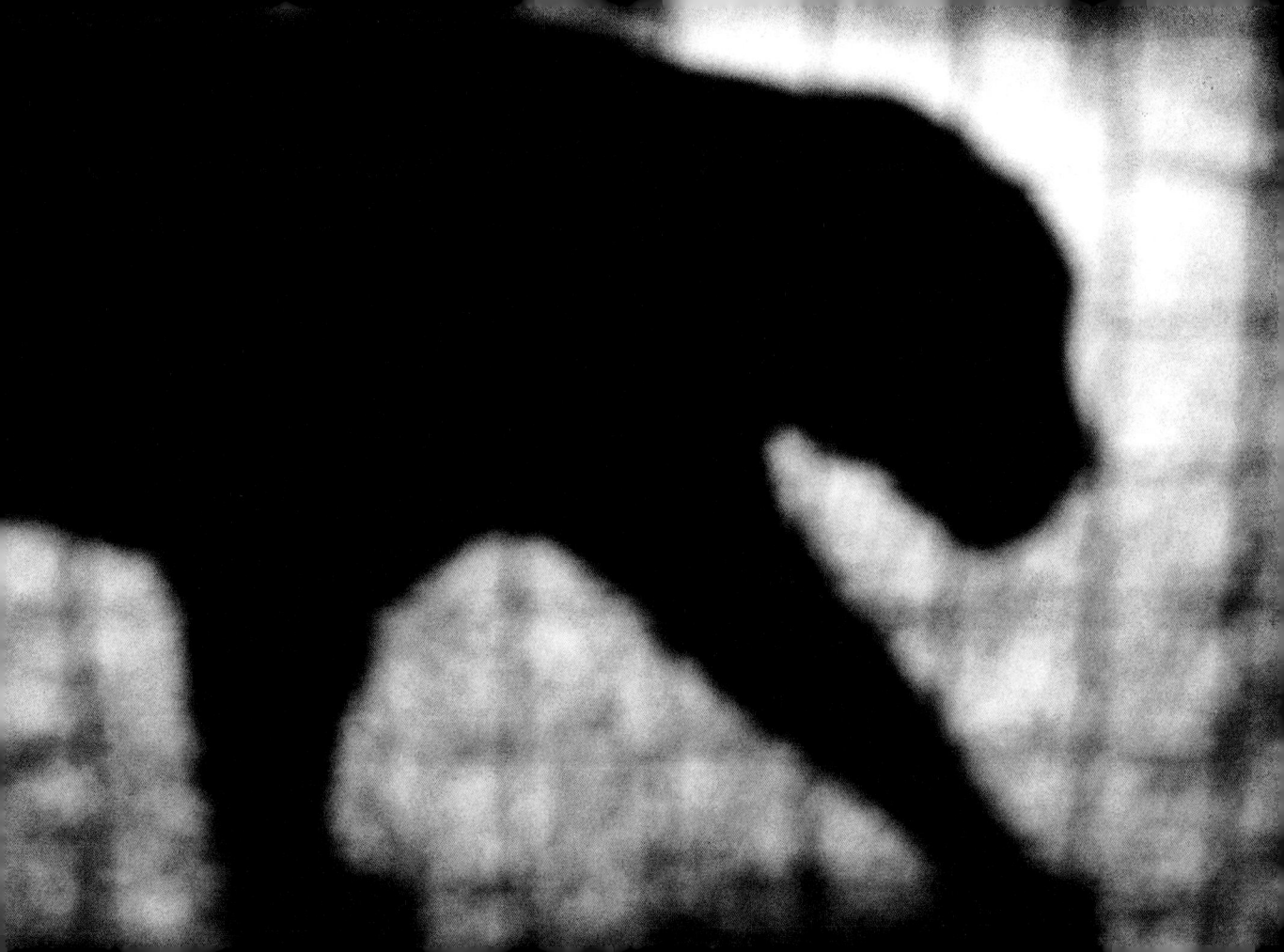

29. Chessington 1994

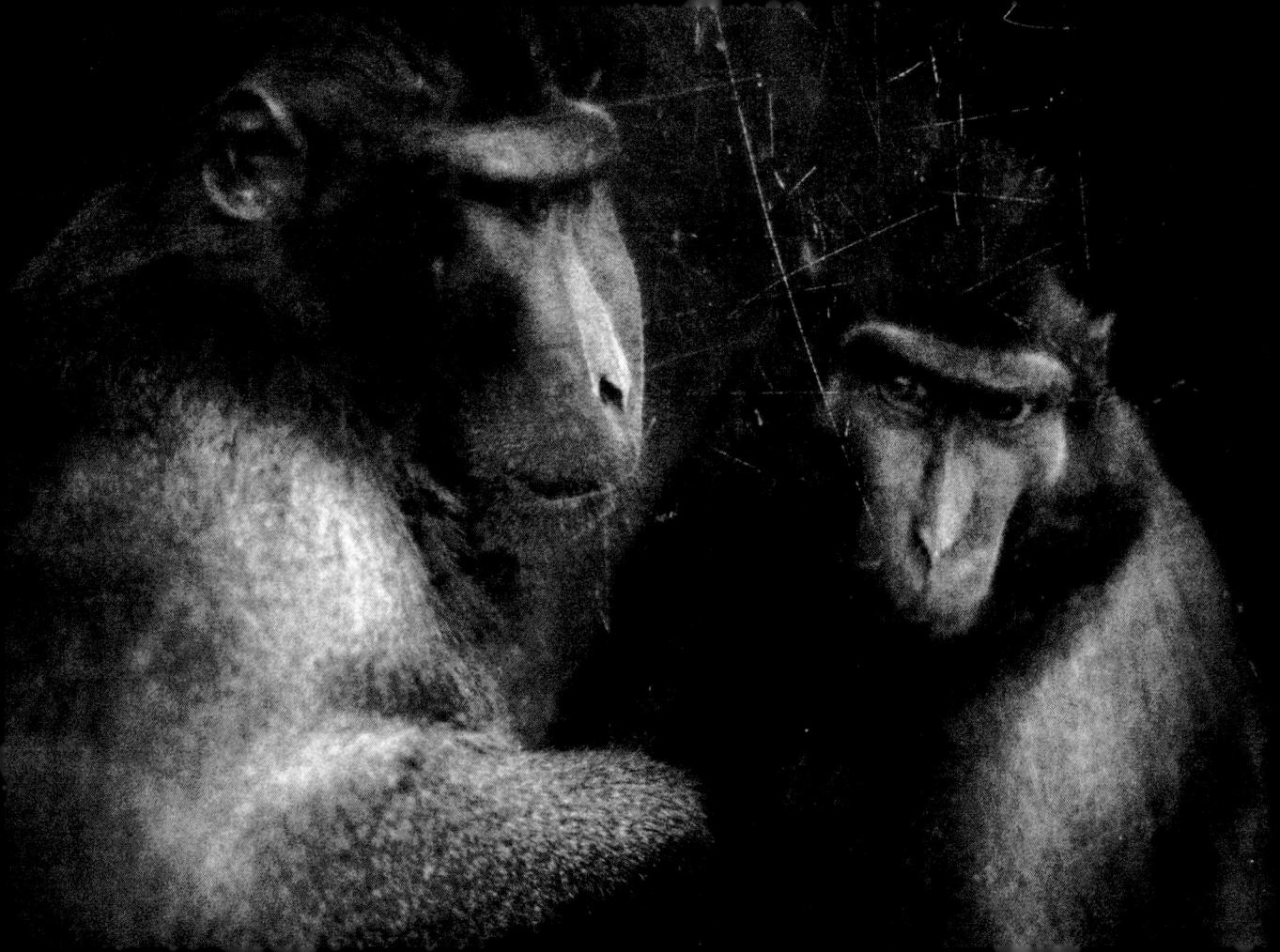

30. Chessington 1994

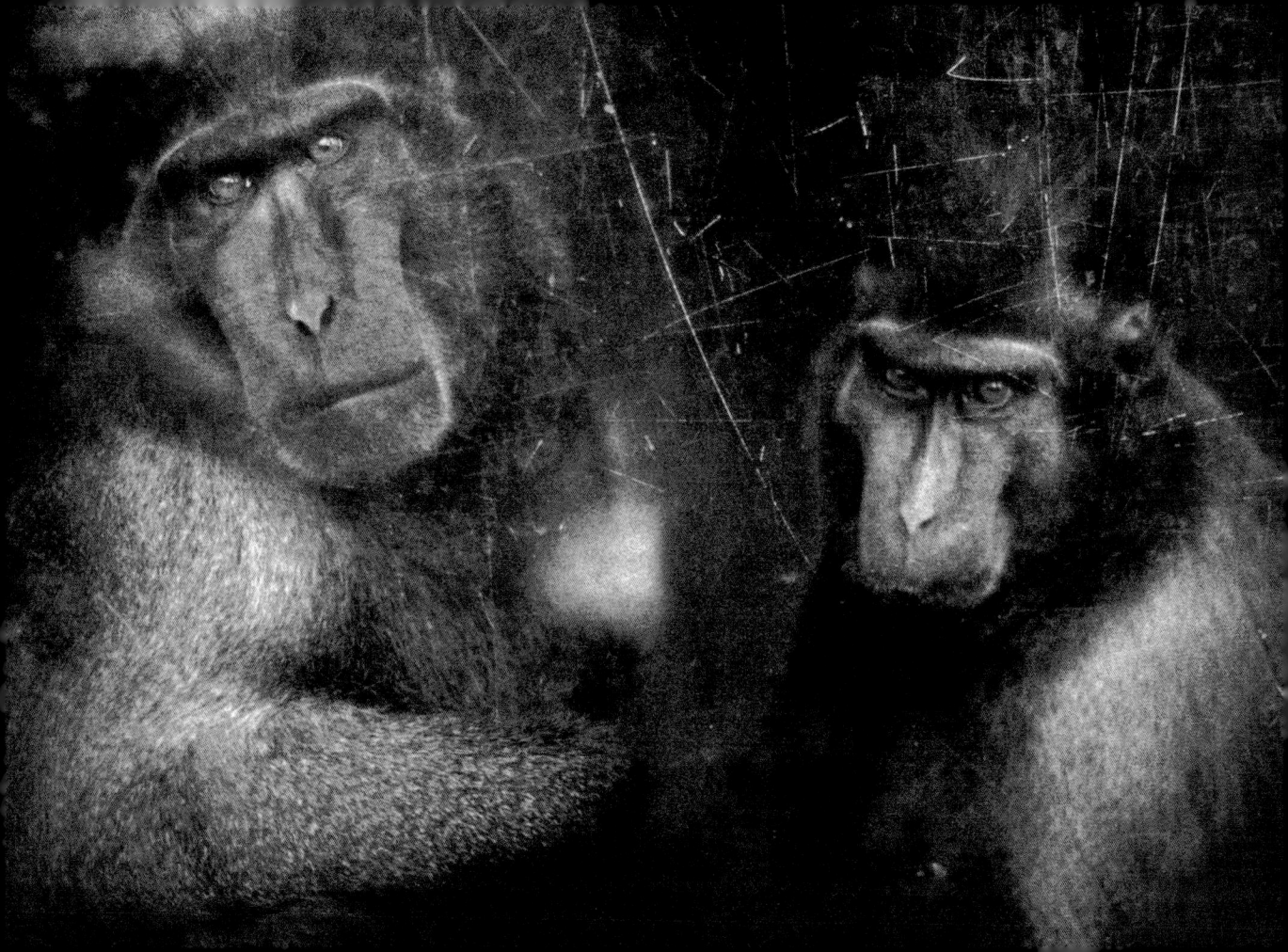

31. Los Angeles 1995

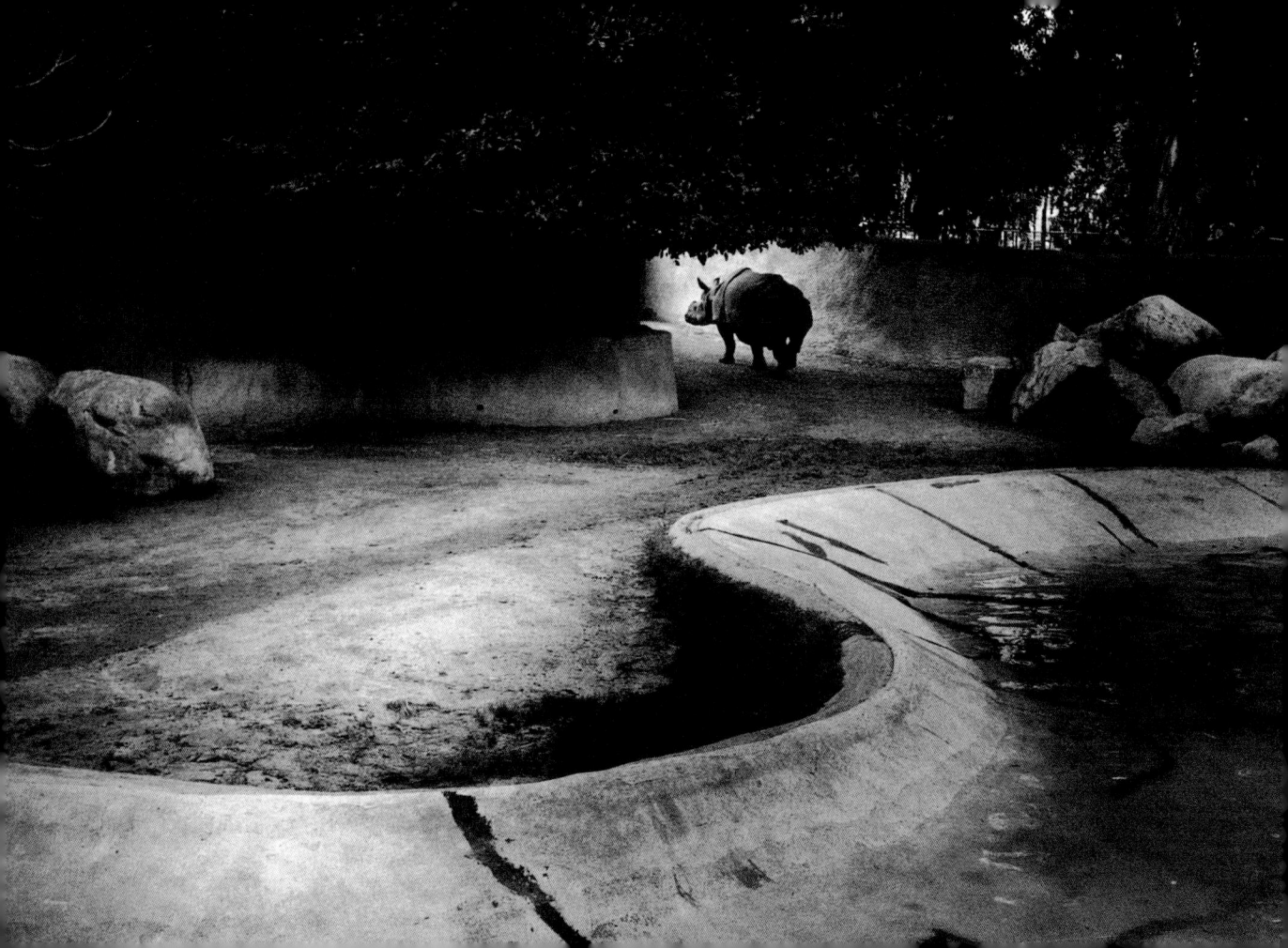

32. Winchester 1994

33. Berlin 1992

34. London 1994

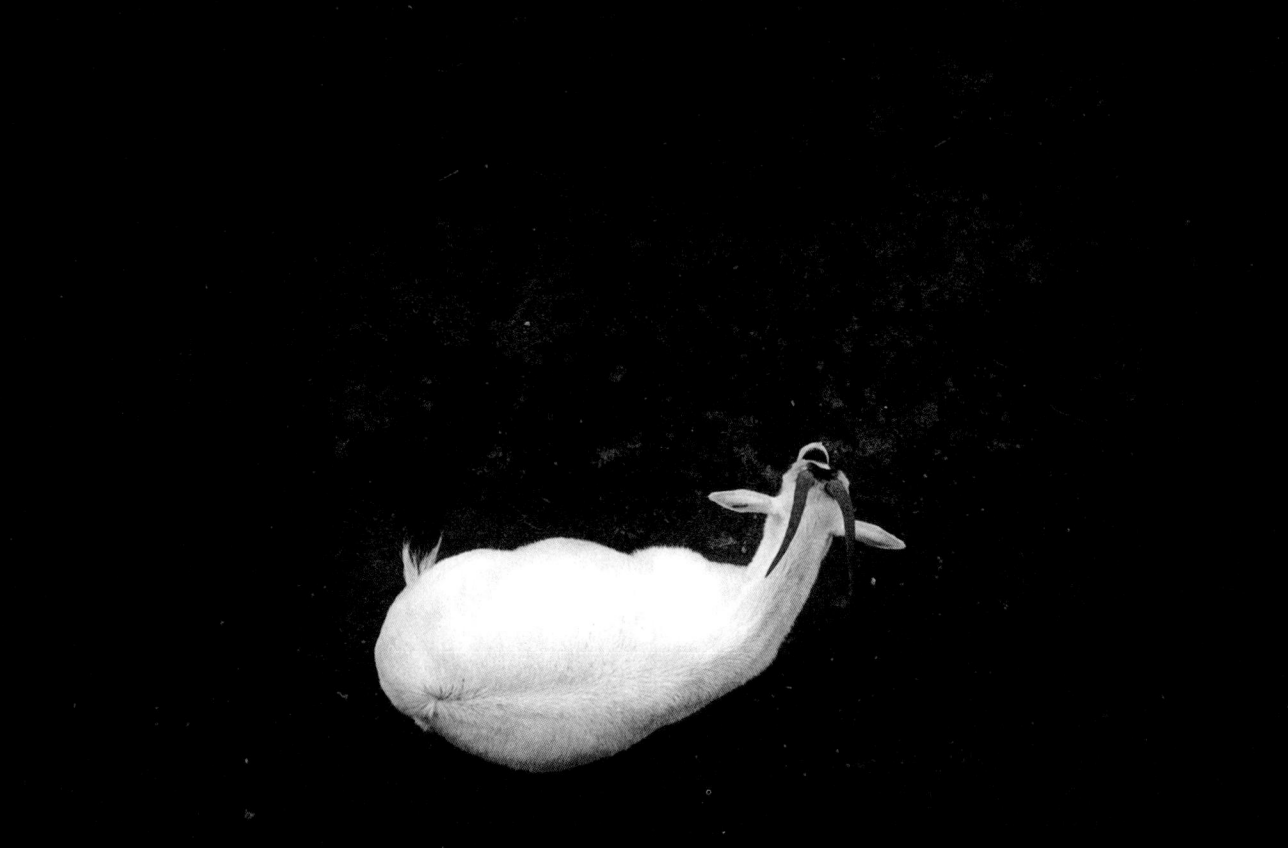

35. Winchester 1994

36. Osnabrück 1994

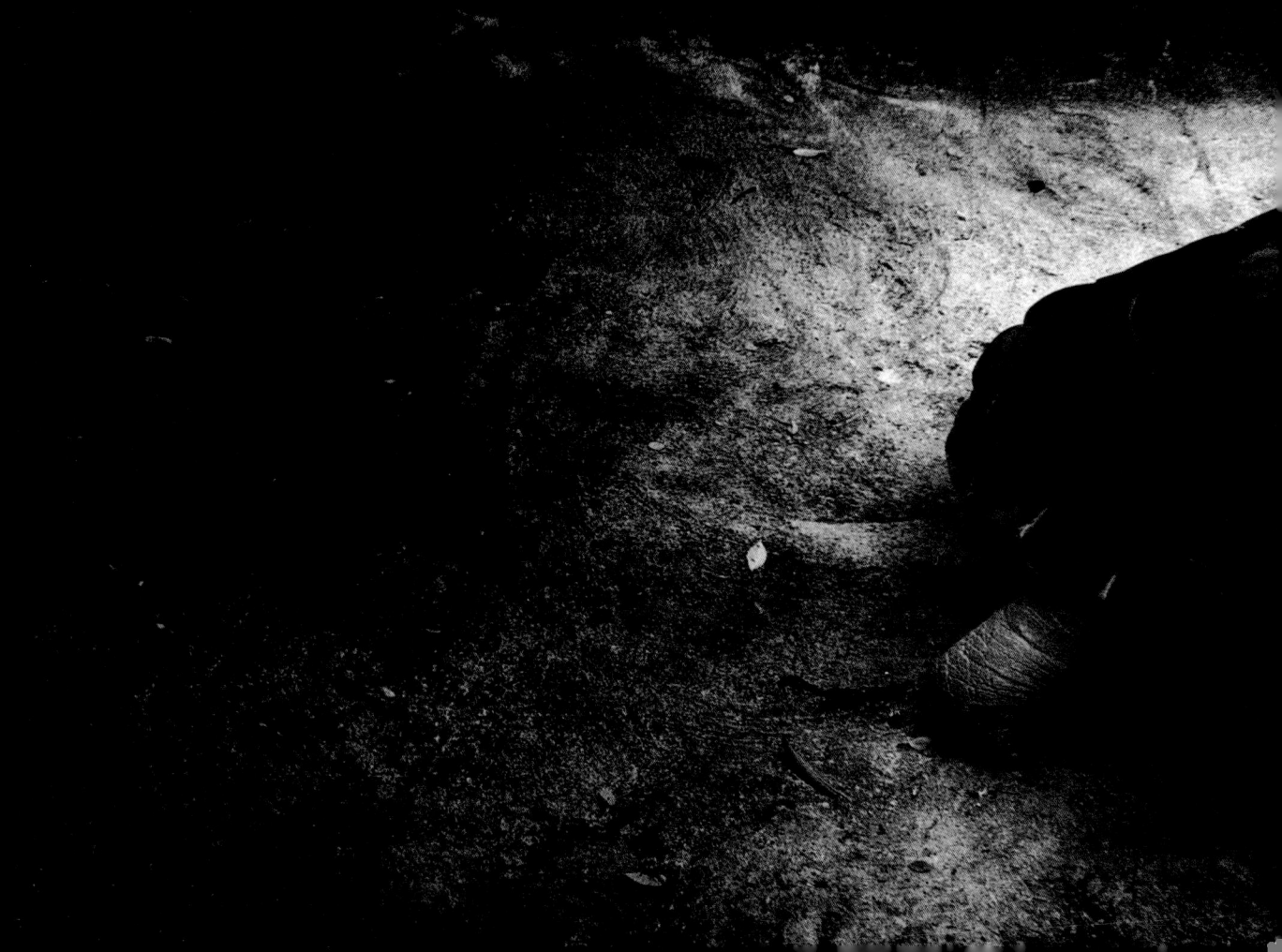

37. Dublin 1992

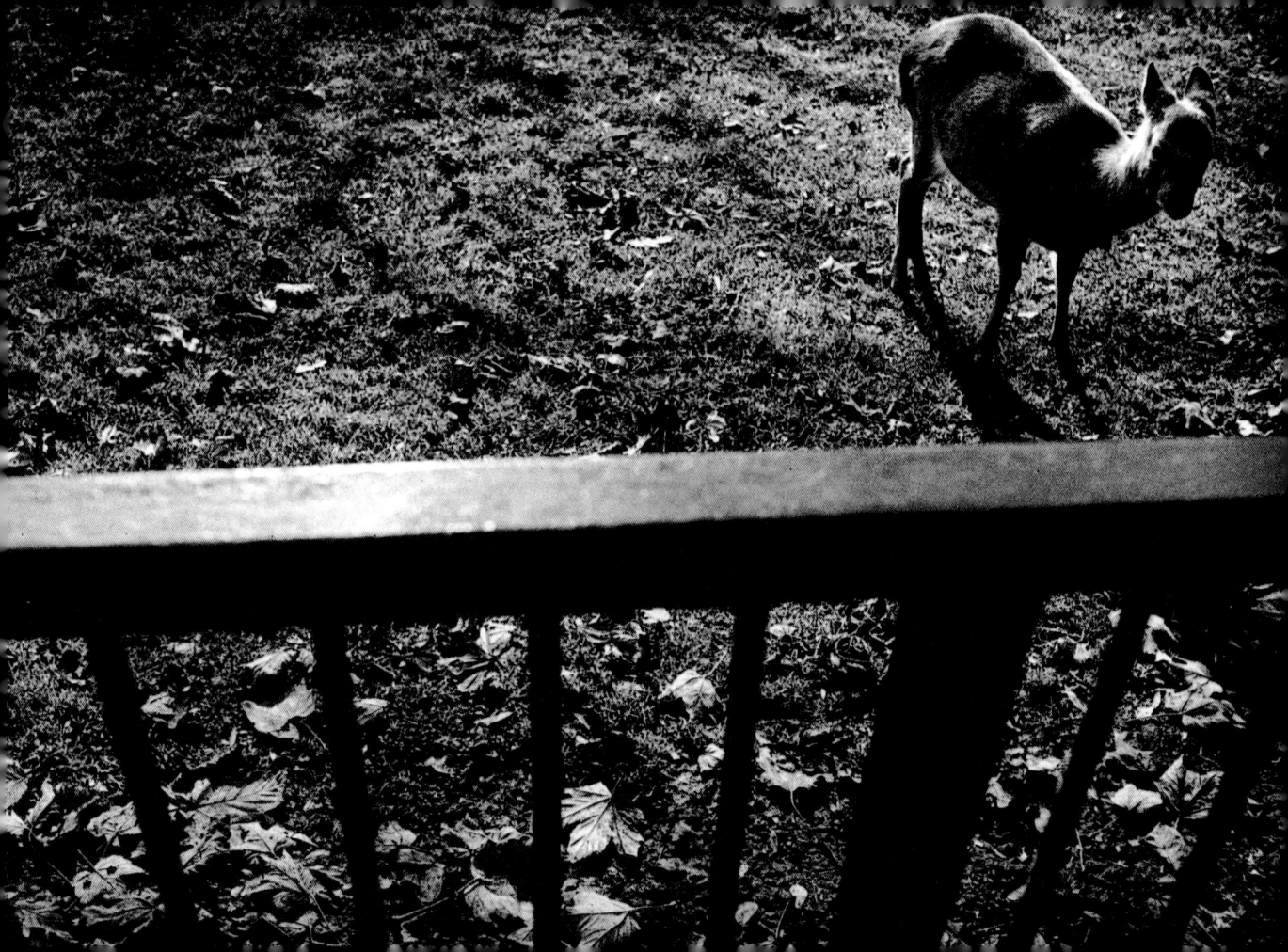

38. London 1992

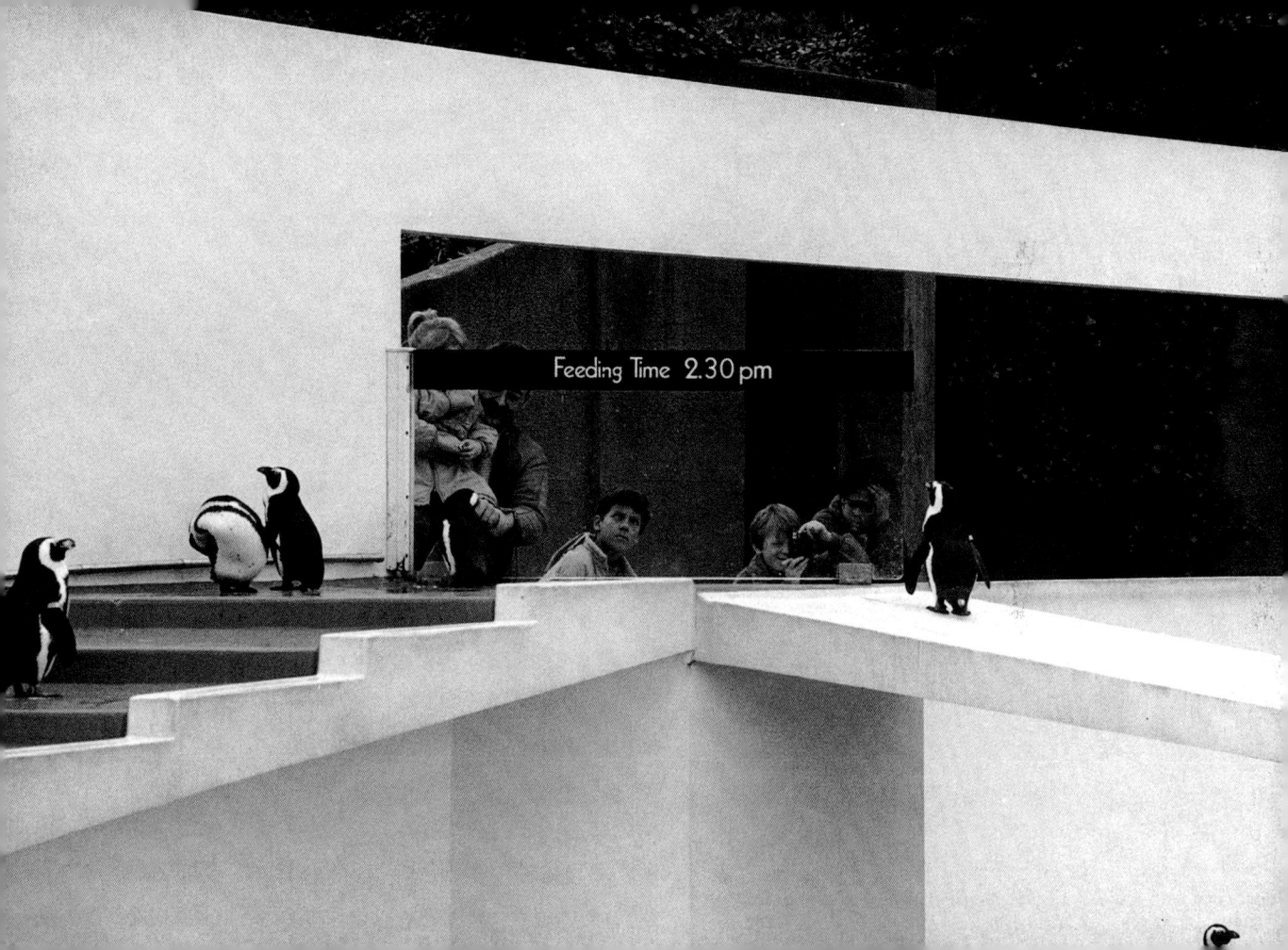

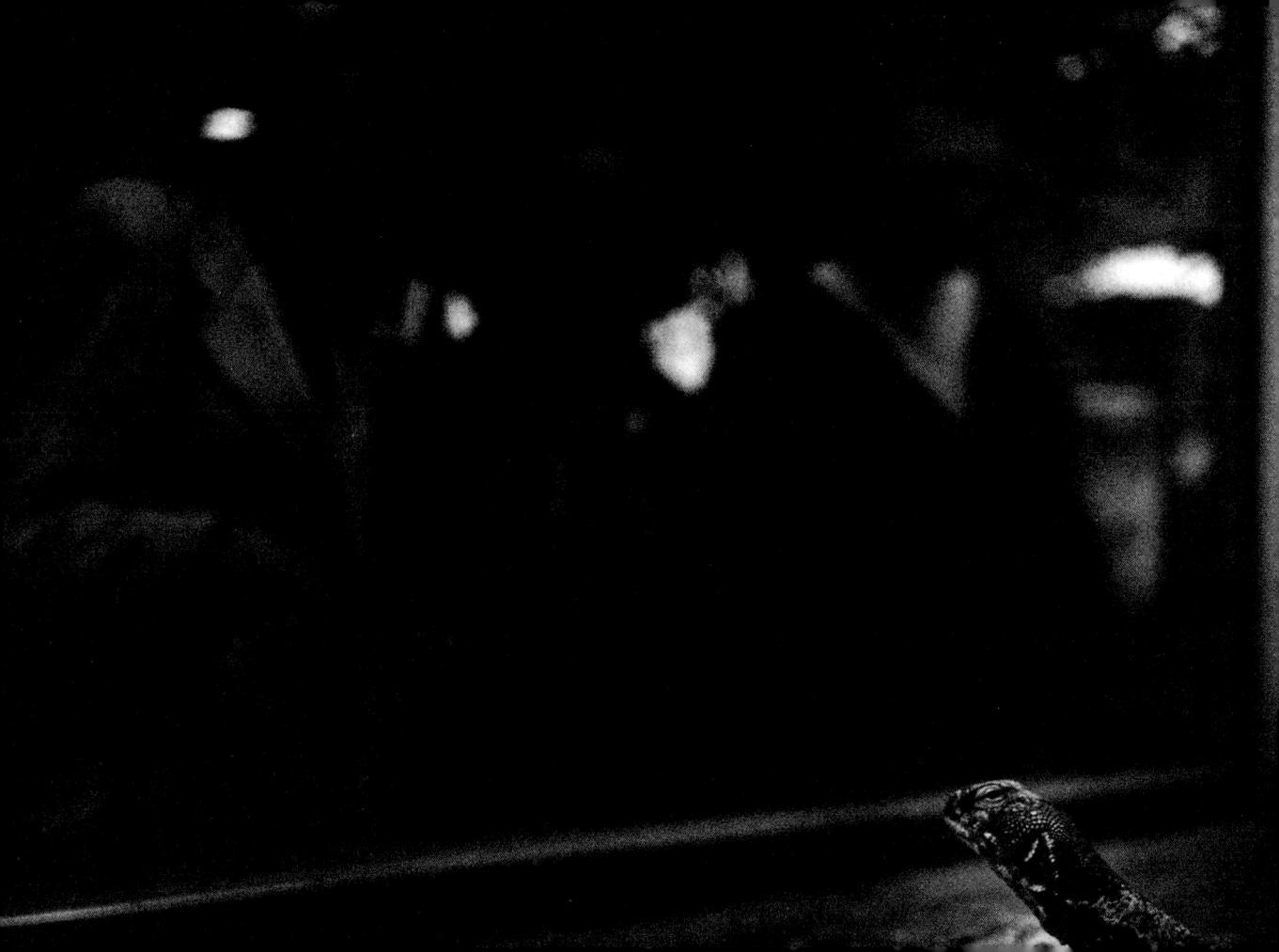

39. Hamburg 1994

40, 41, 42. New York 1995

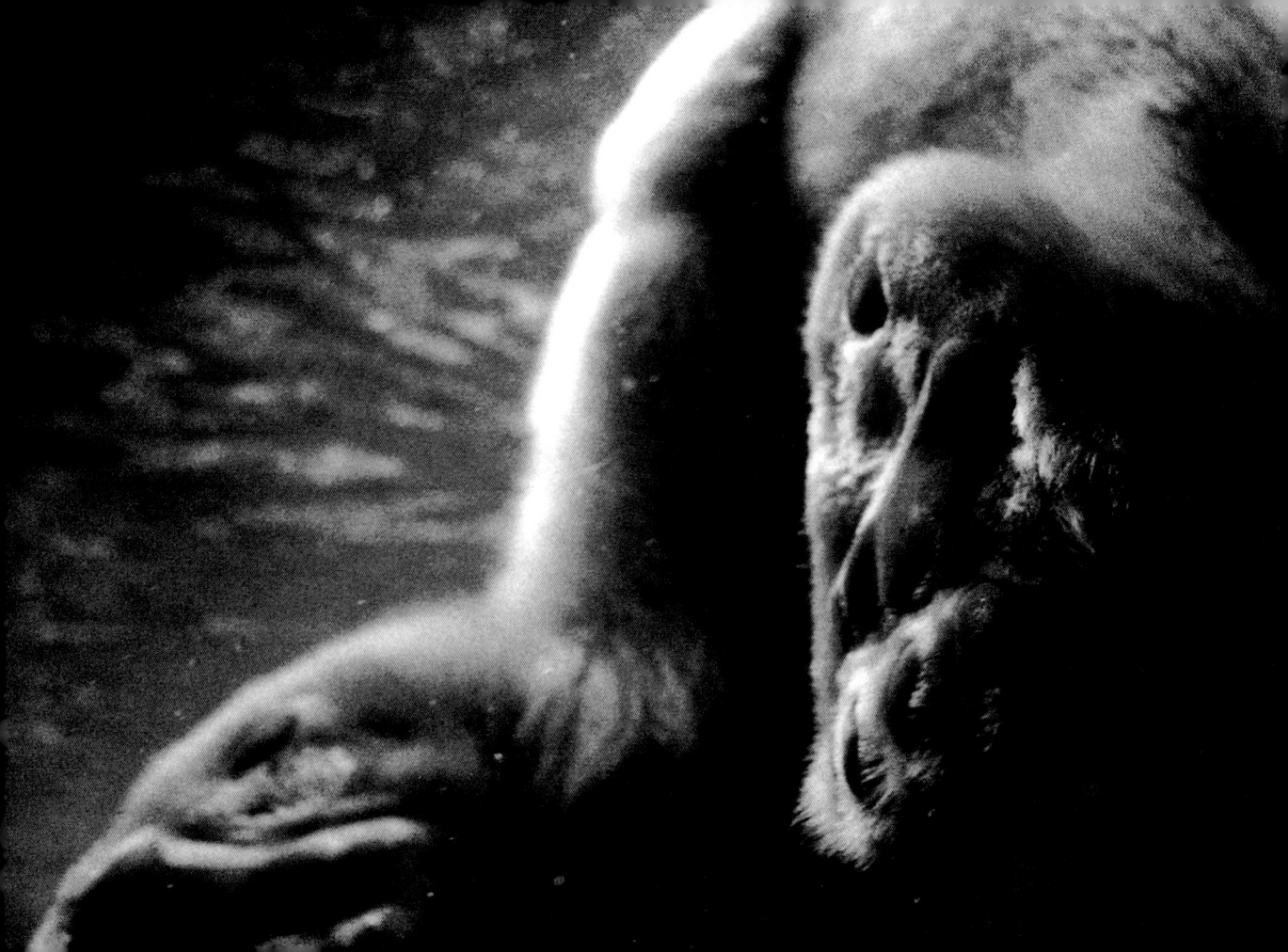

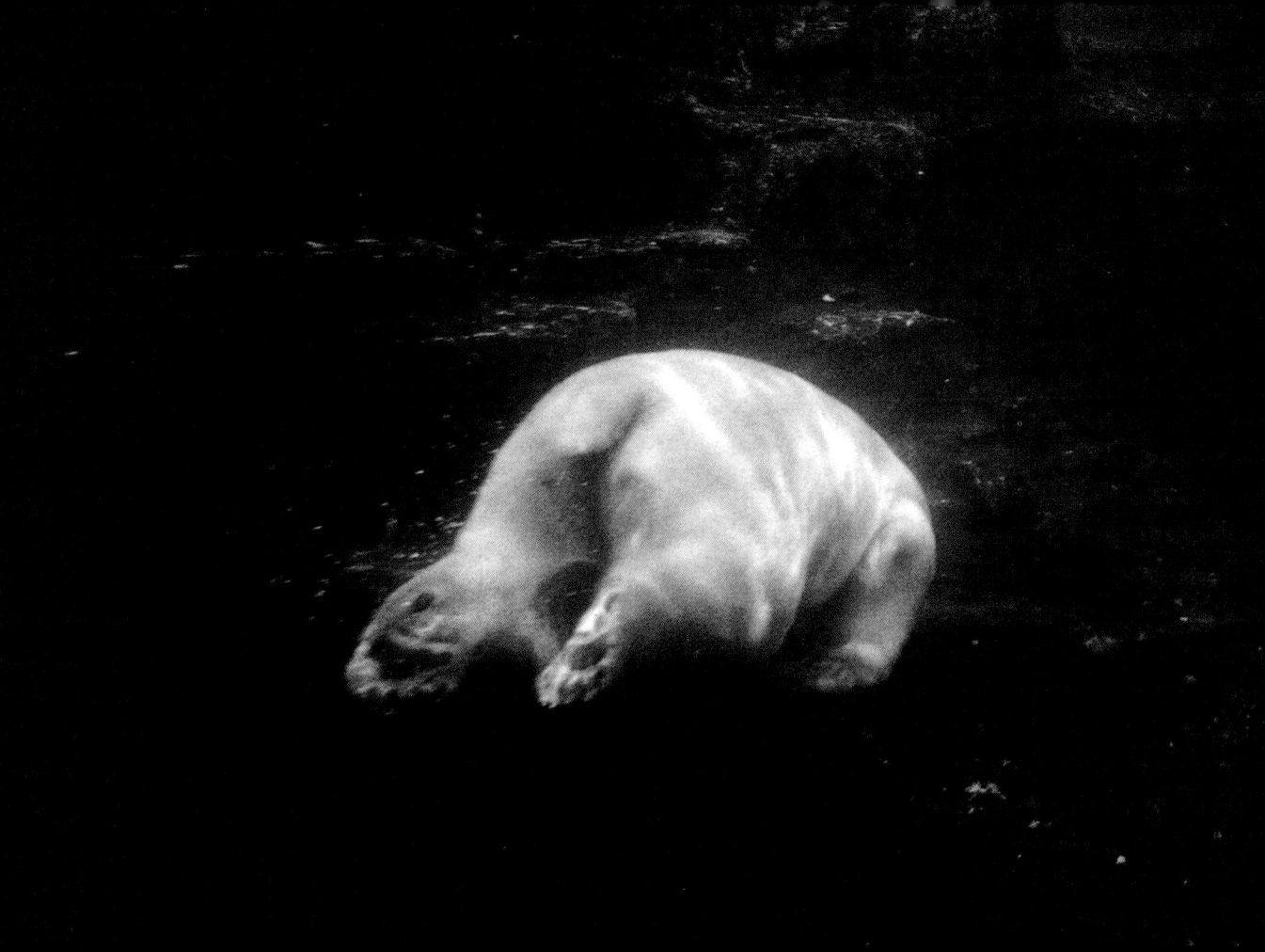

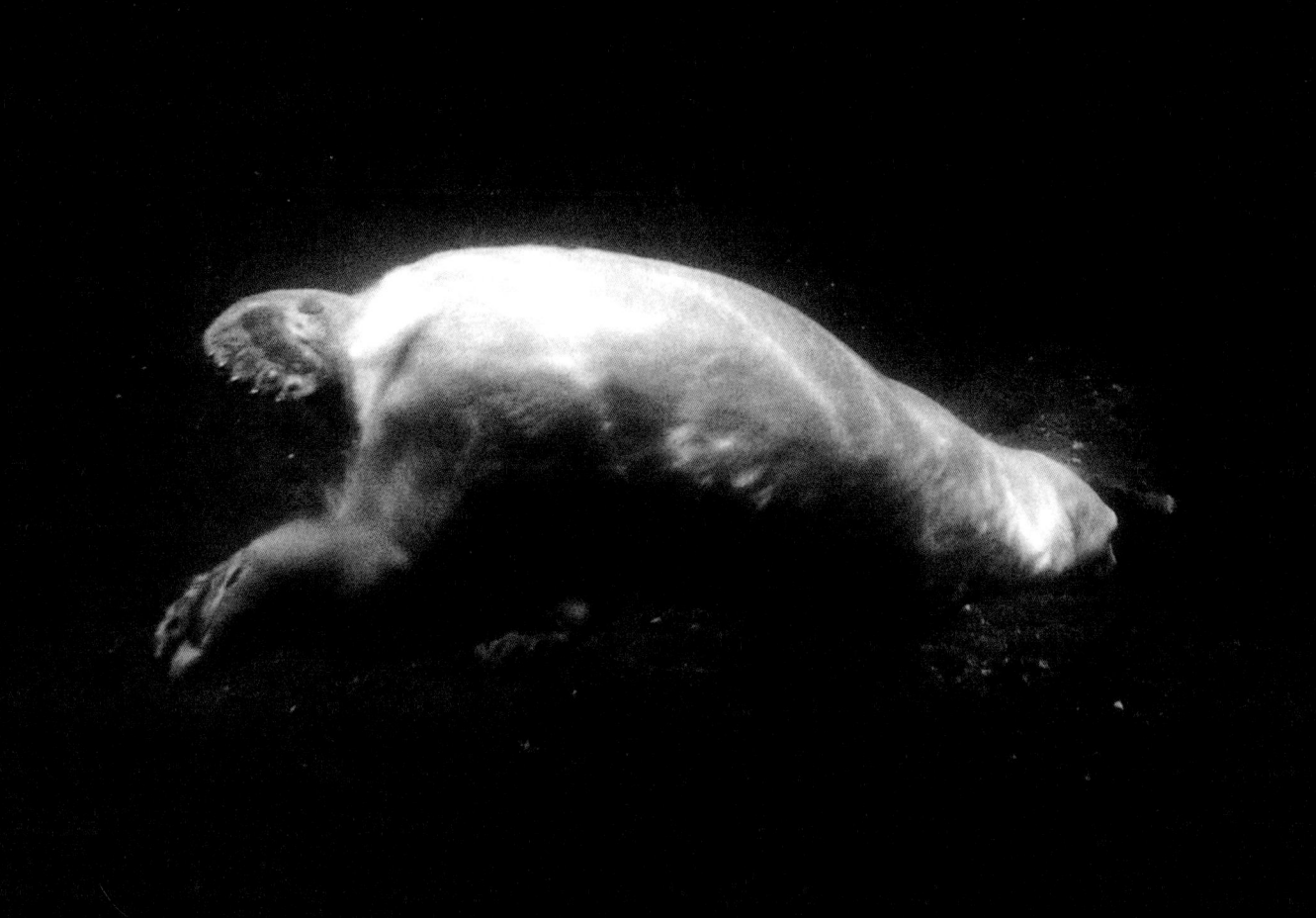

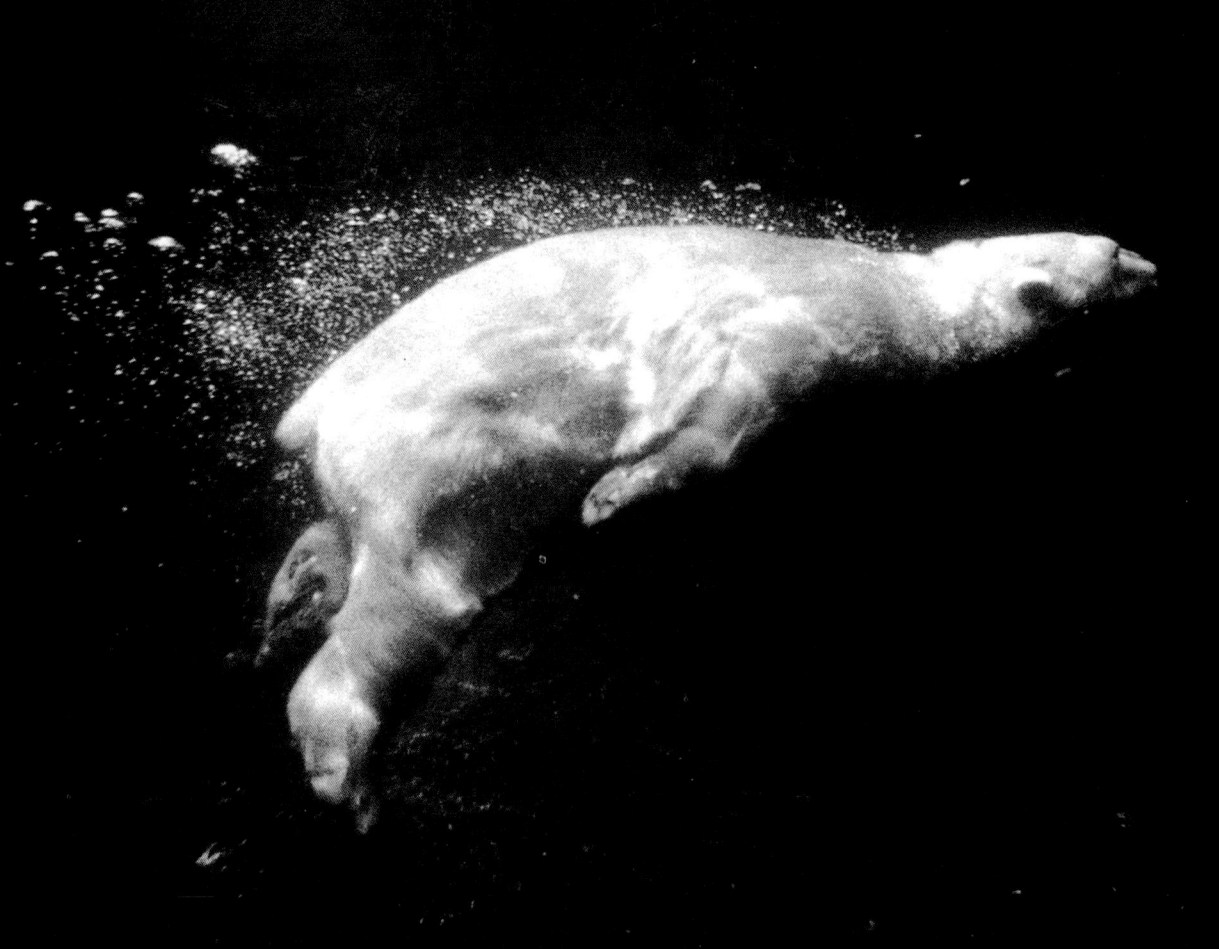

43. New York 1995

44. Bremerhaven 1993

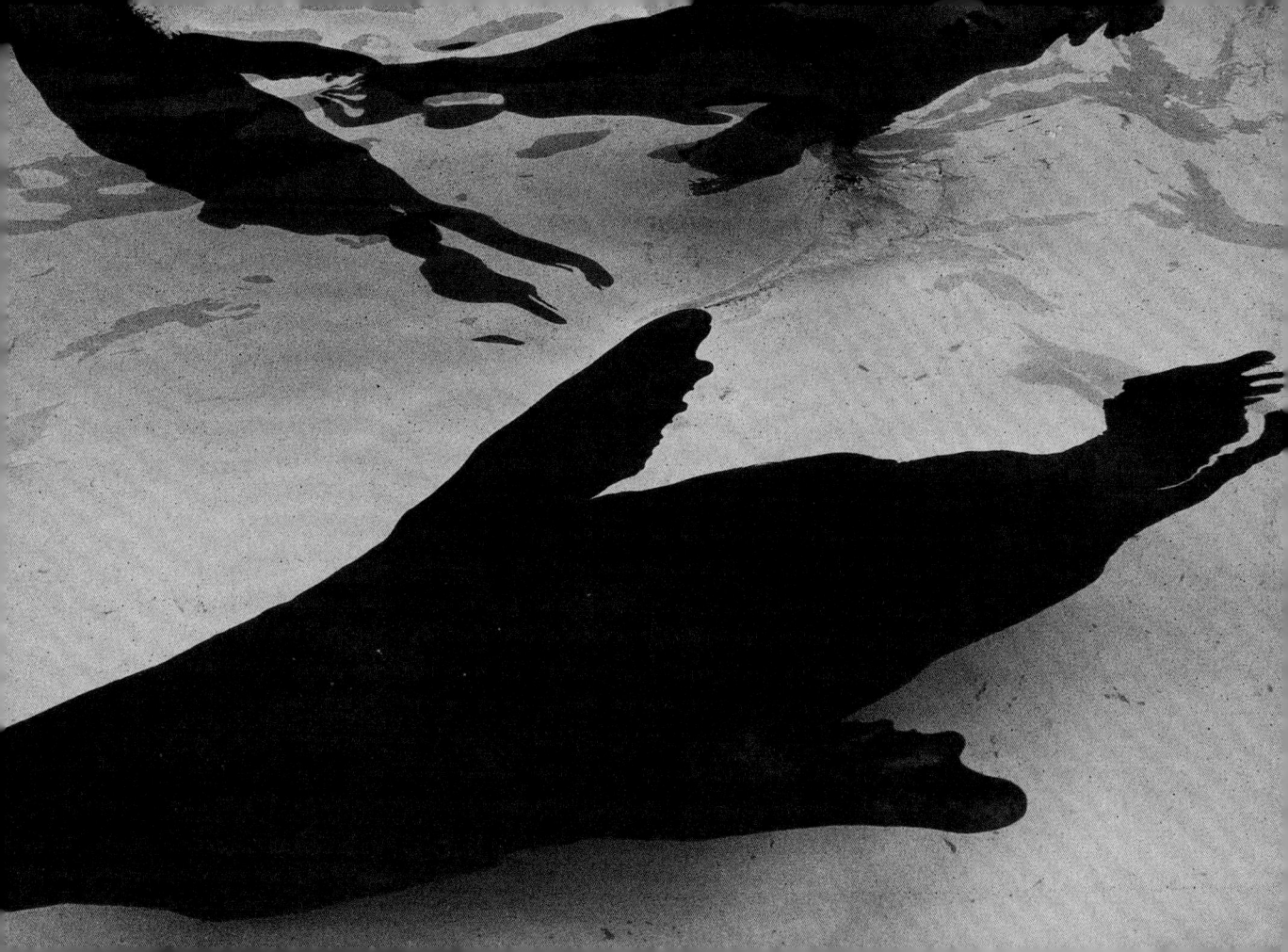

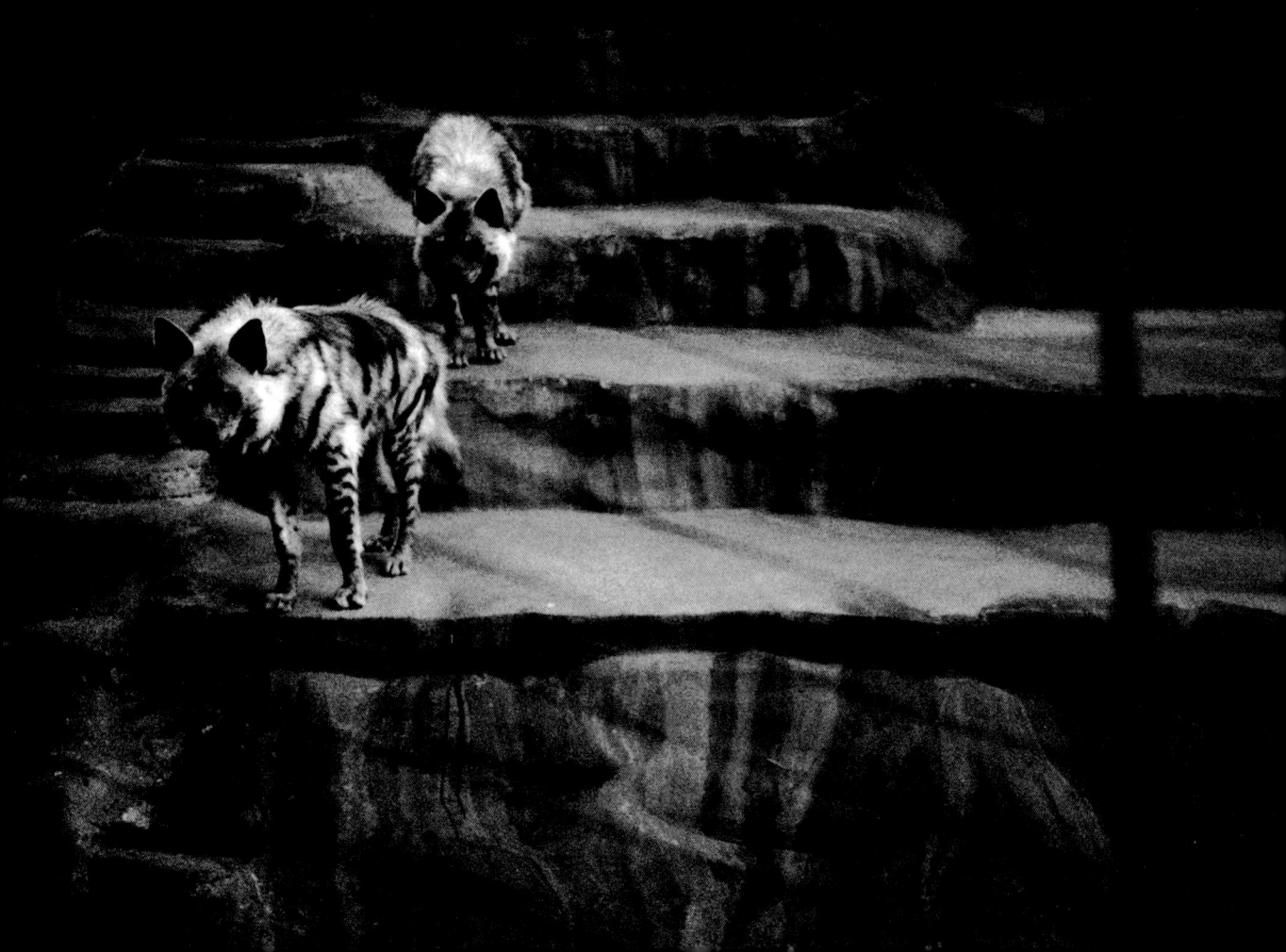

45. San Diego 1995

46. London 1993

47. London 1993

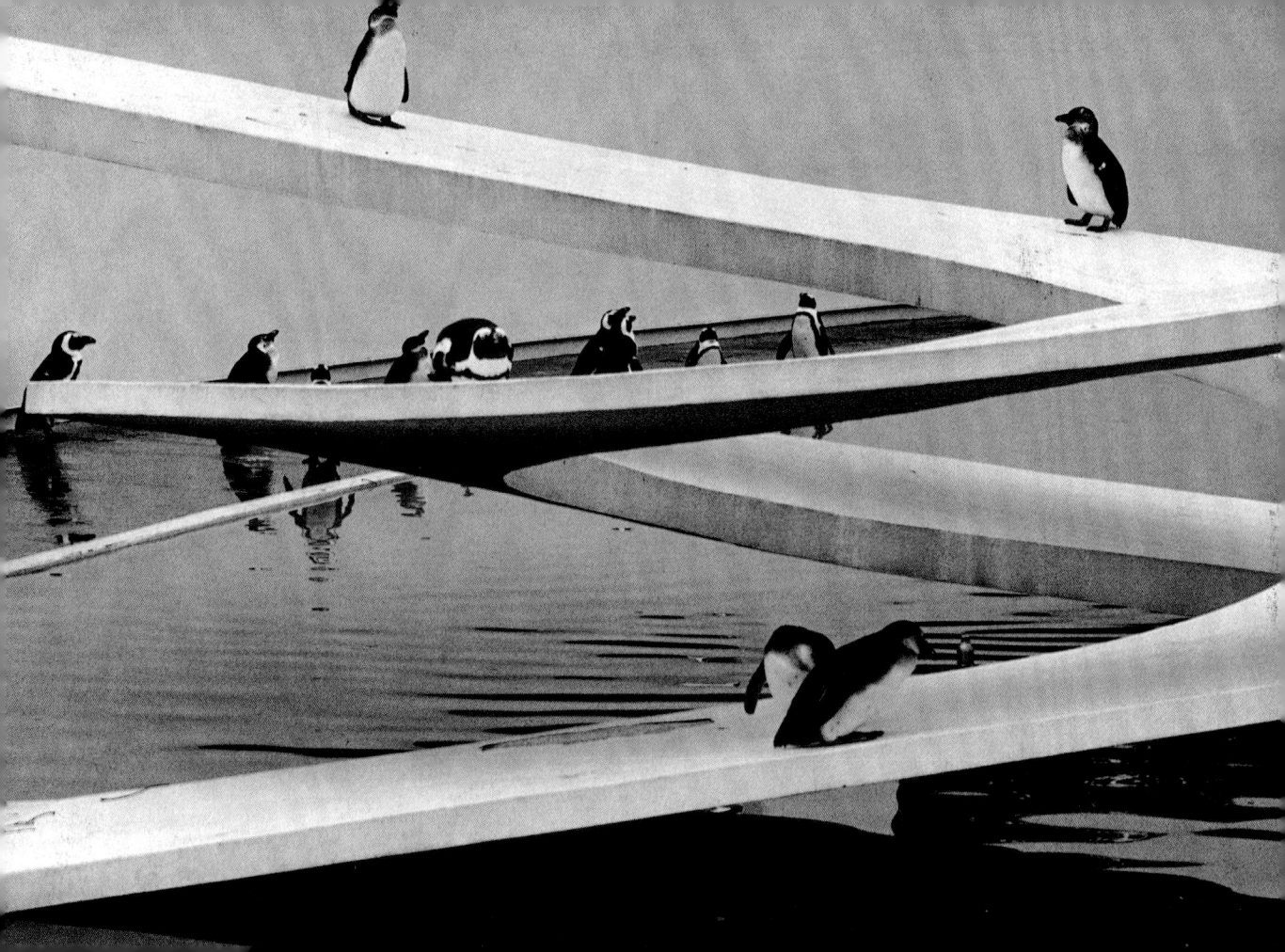

48. Osnabrück 1994

49. Berlin 1992

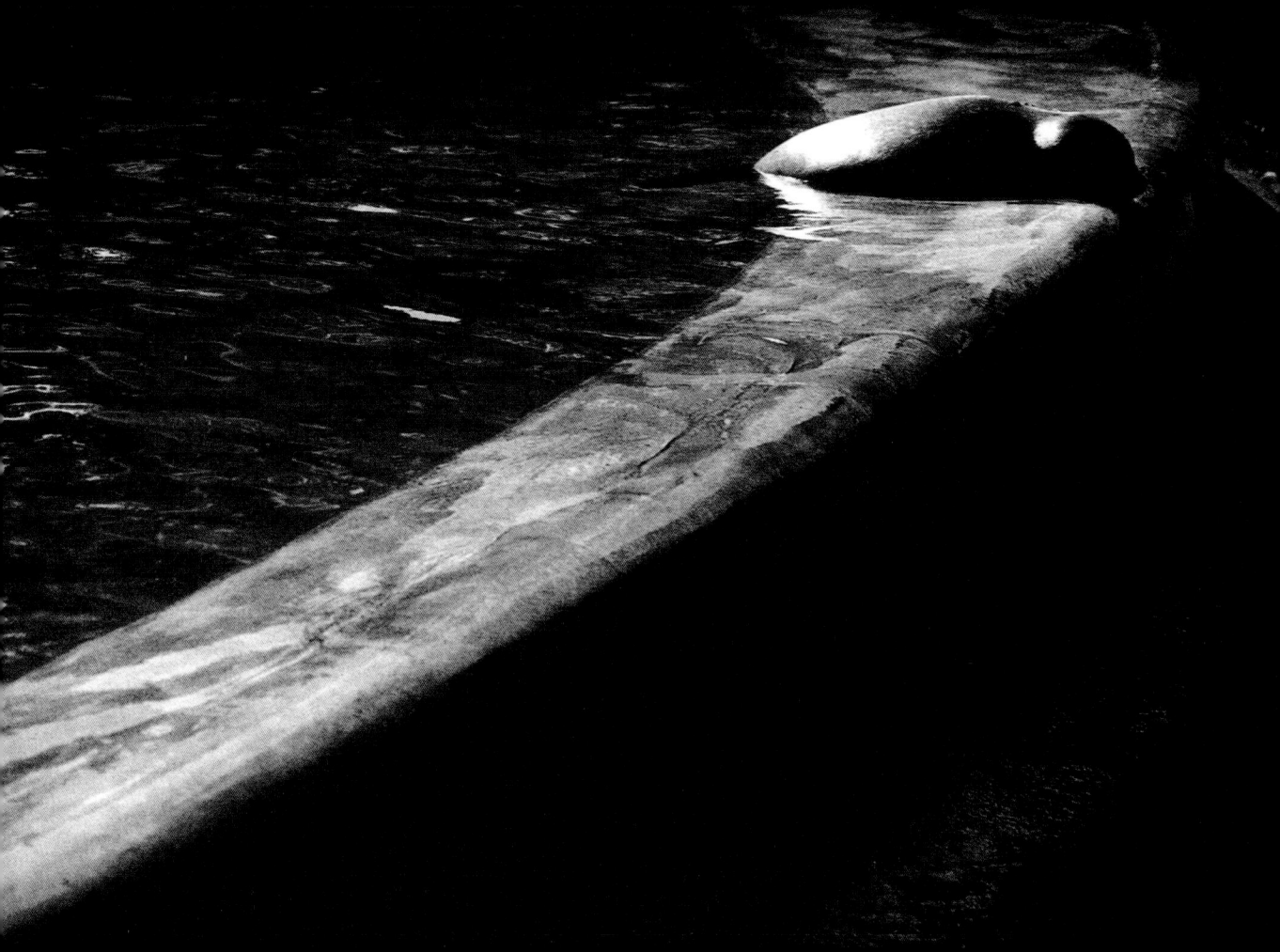

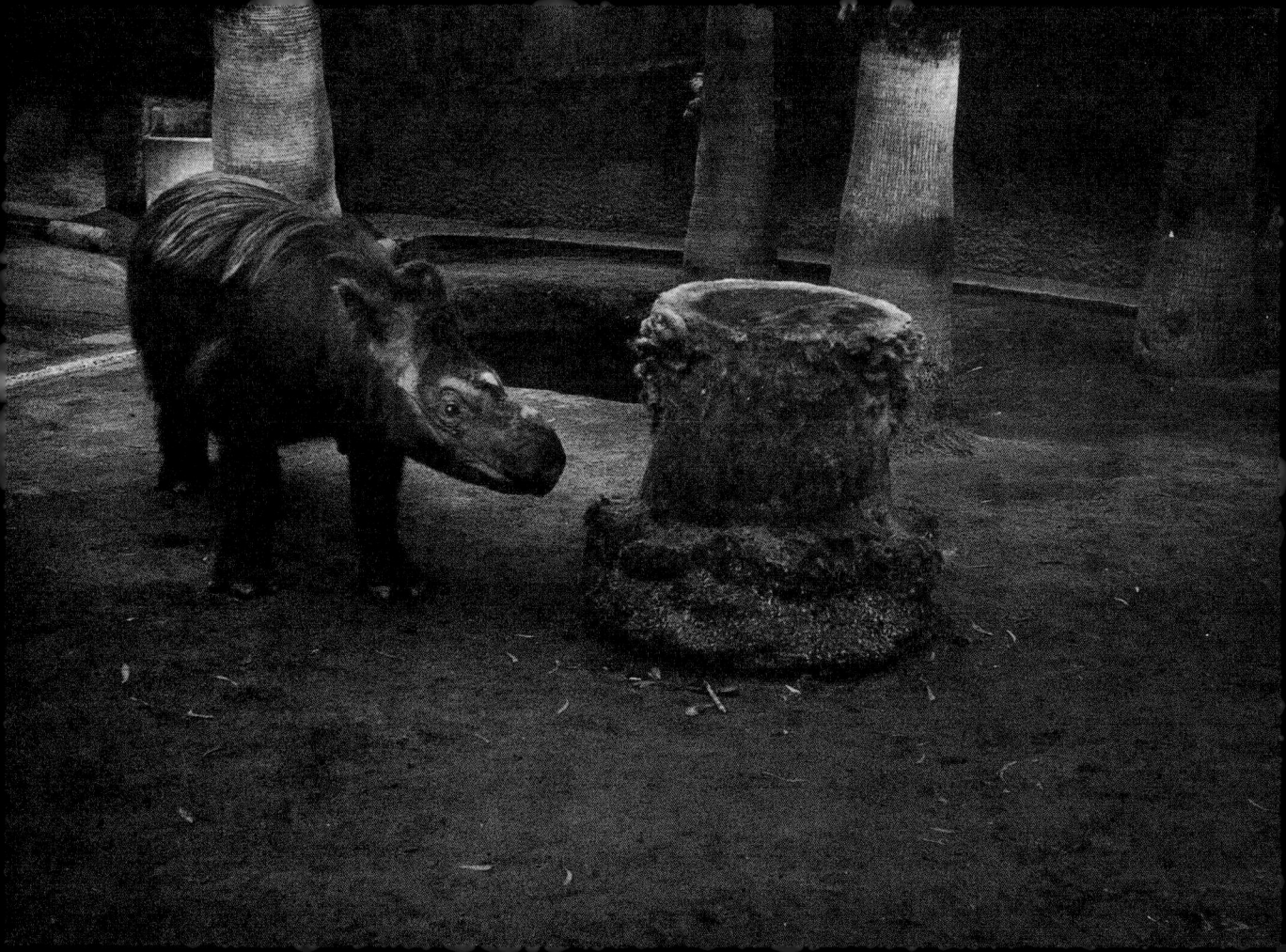

50. San Diego 1995

51. New York 1995

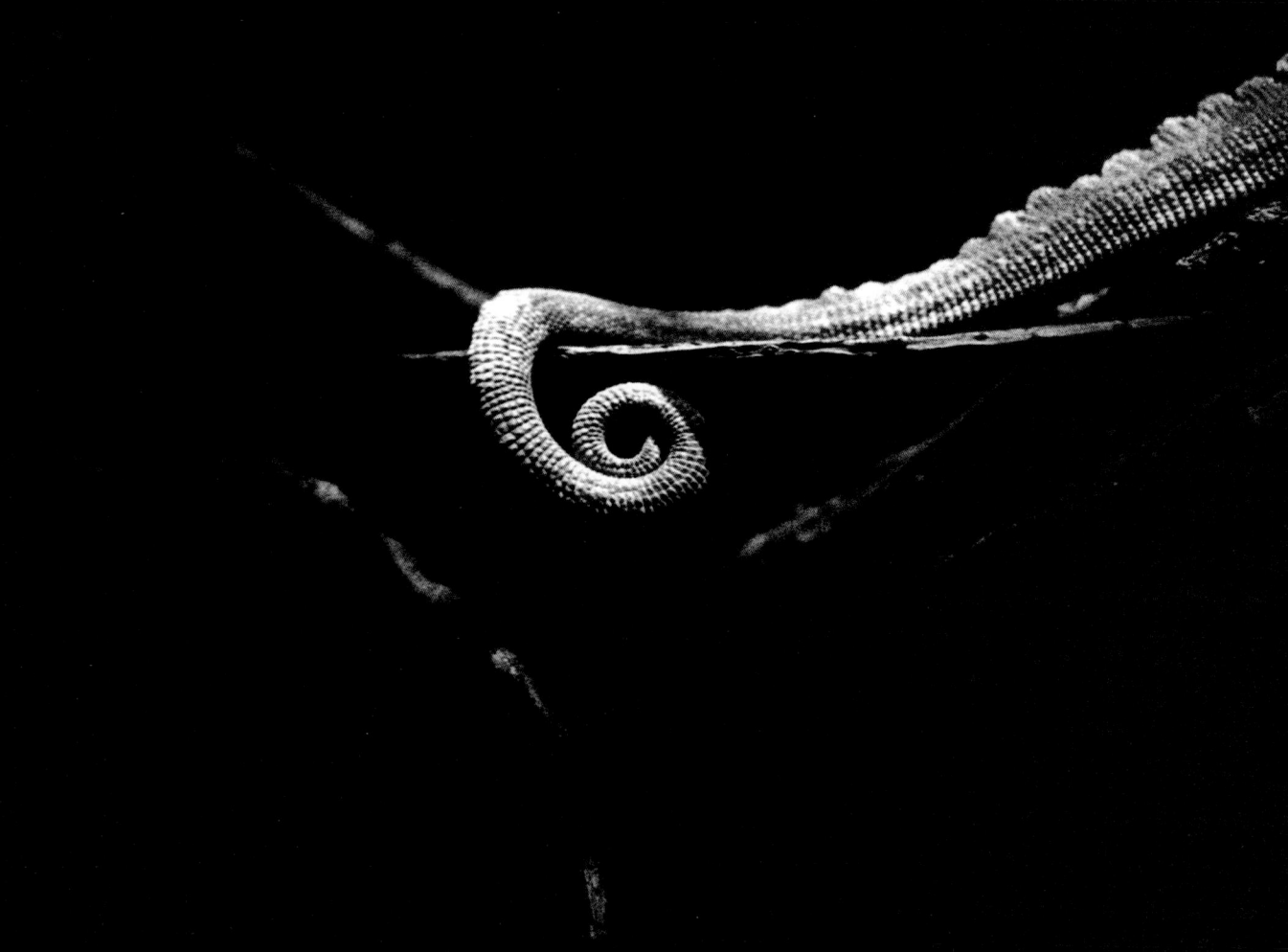

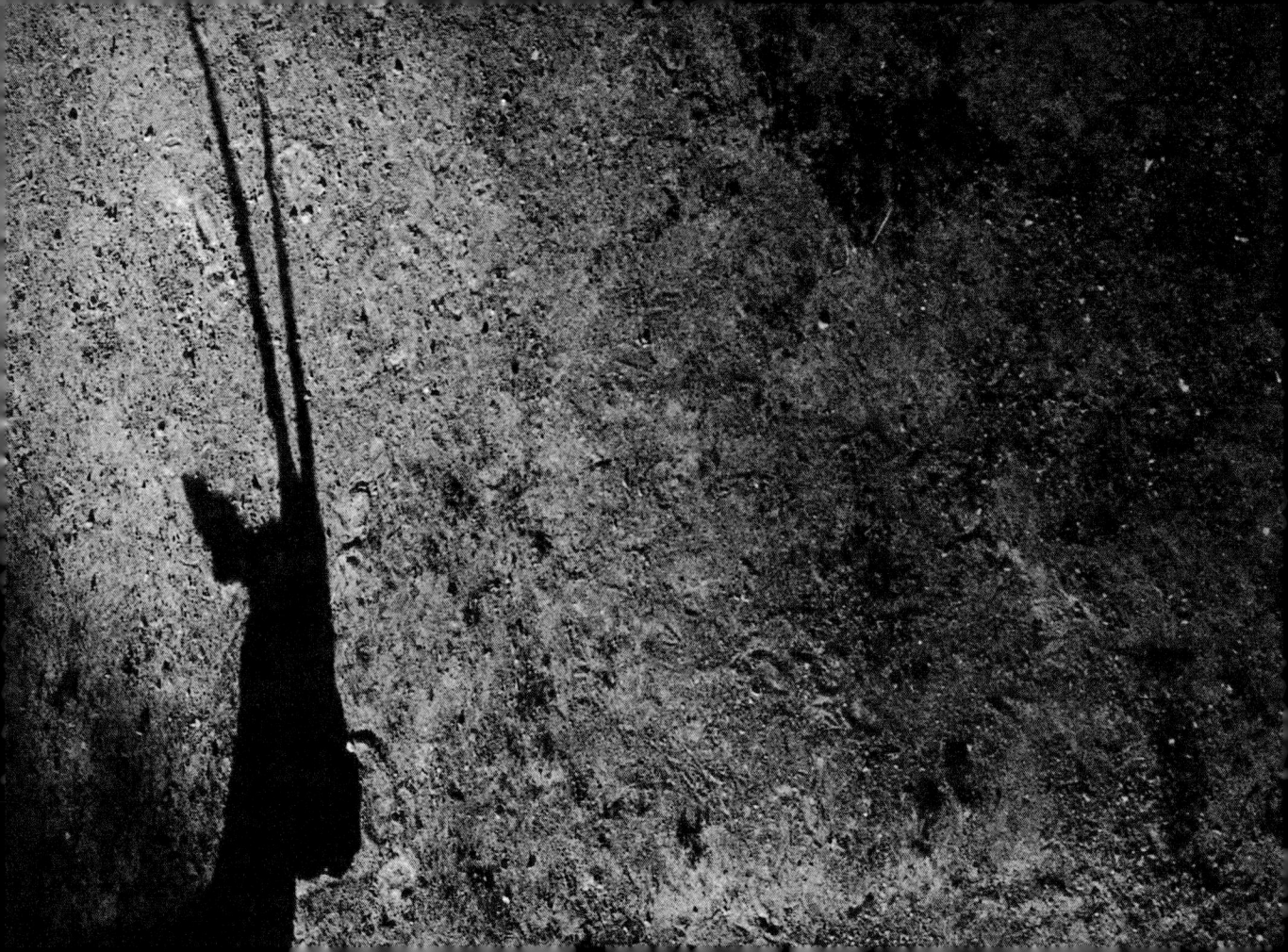

52. London 1994

53. London 1992

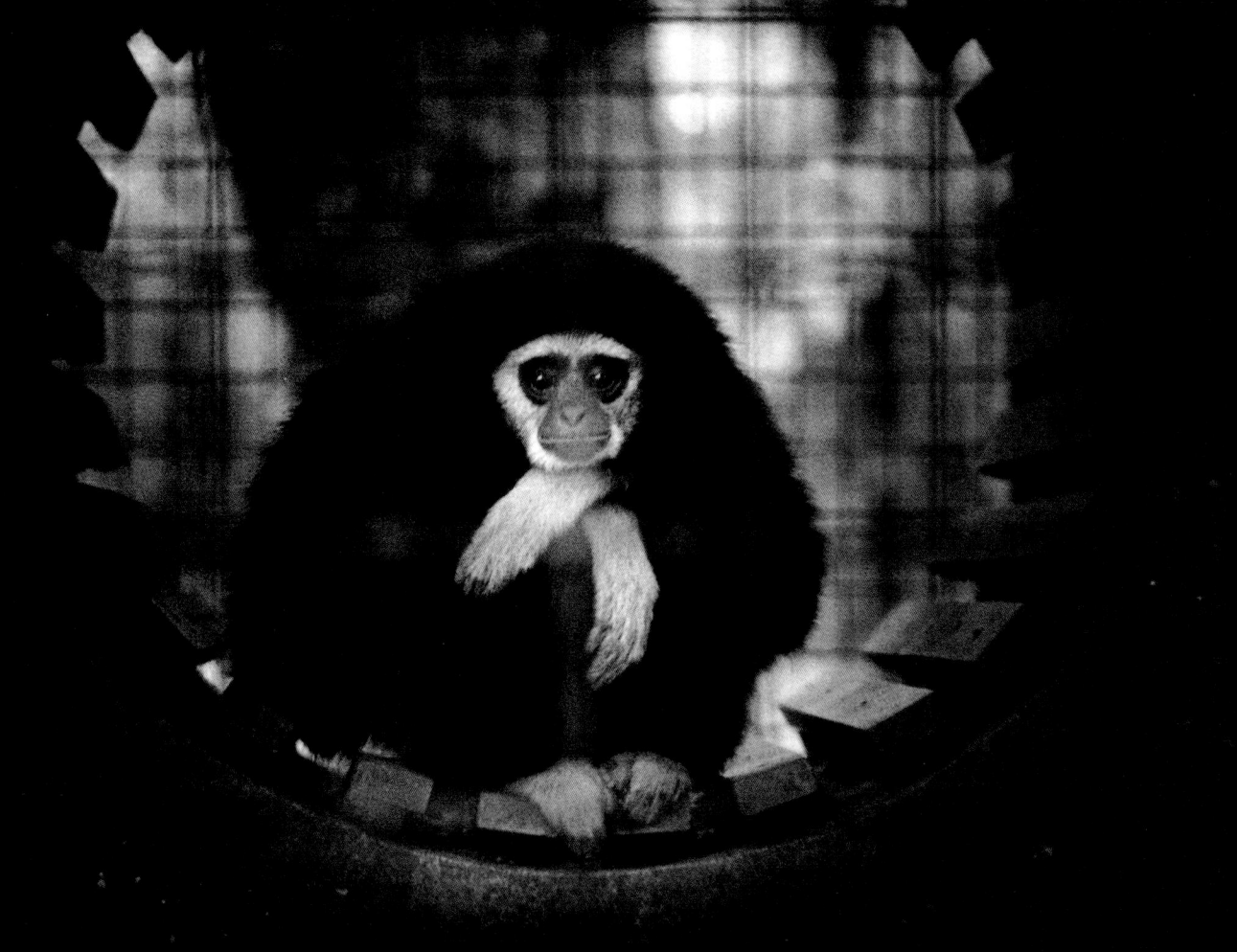

54. London 1992

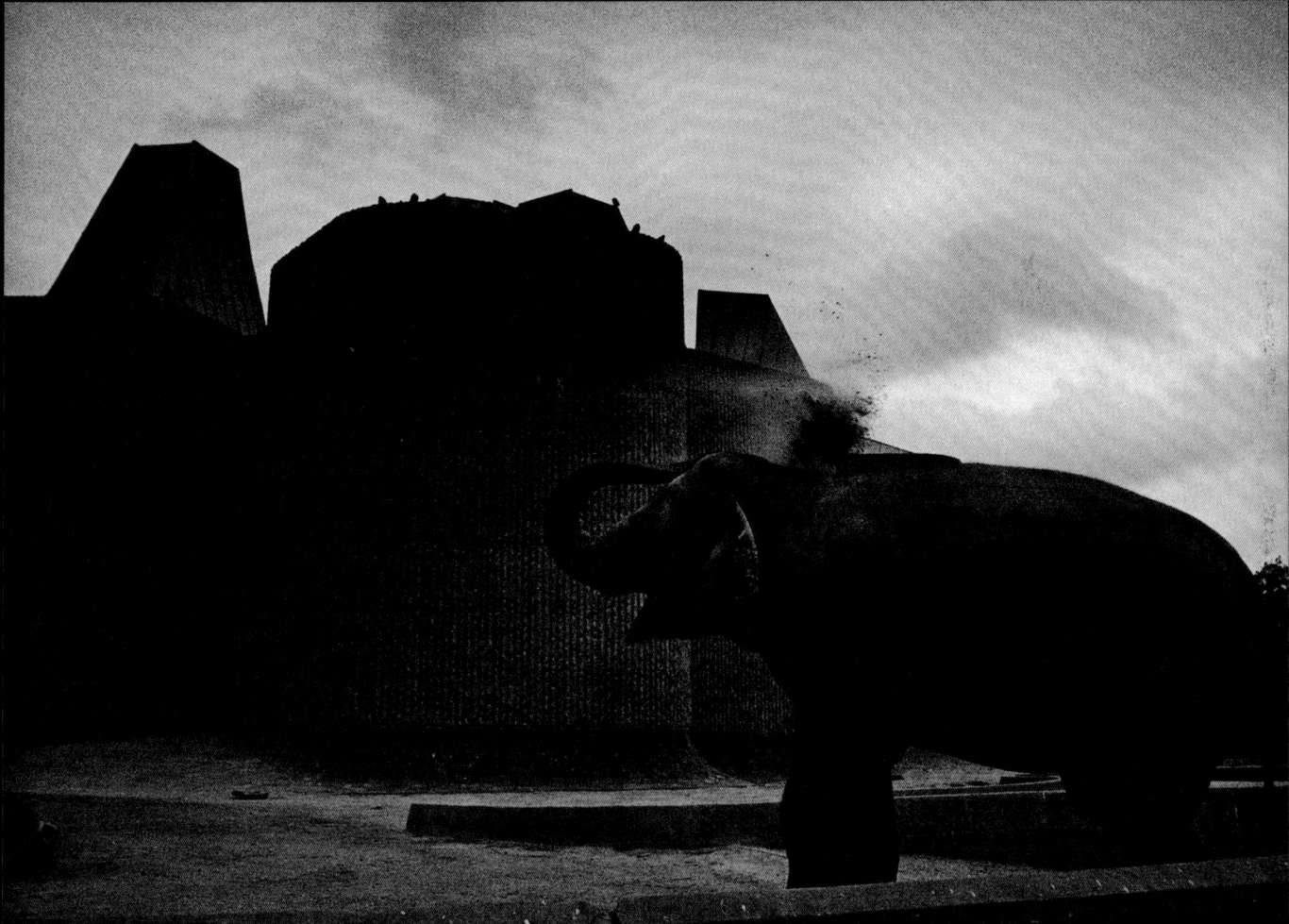

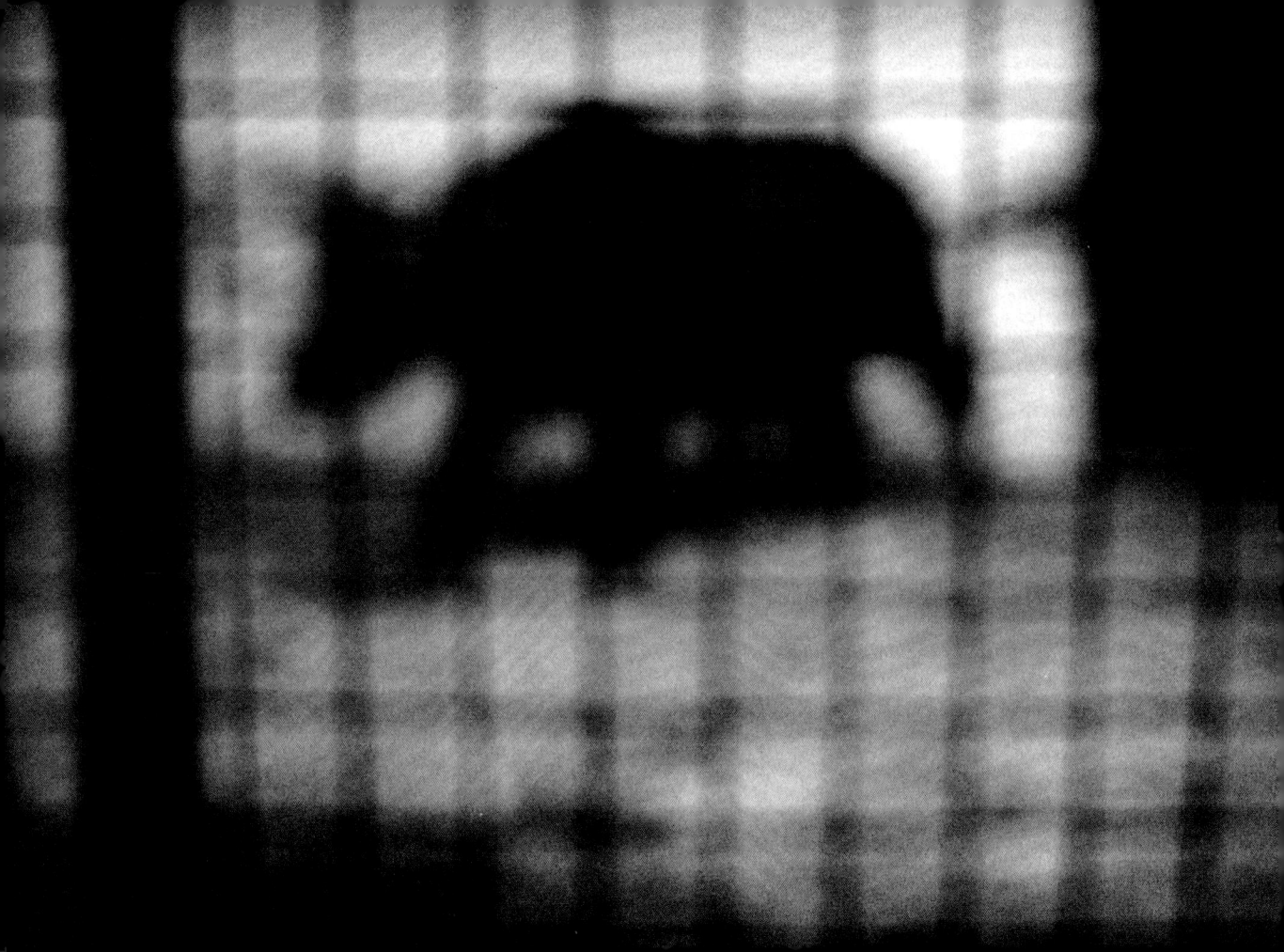

55. Winchester 1994

56. New York 1995

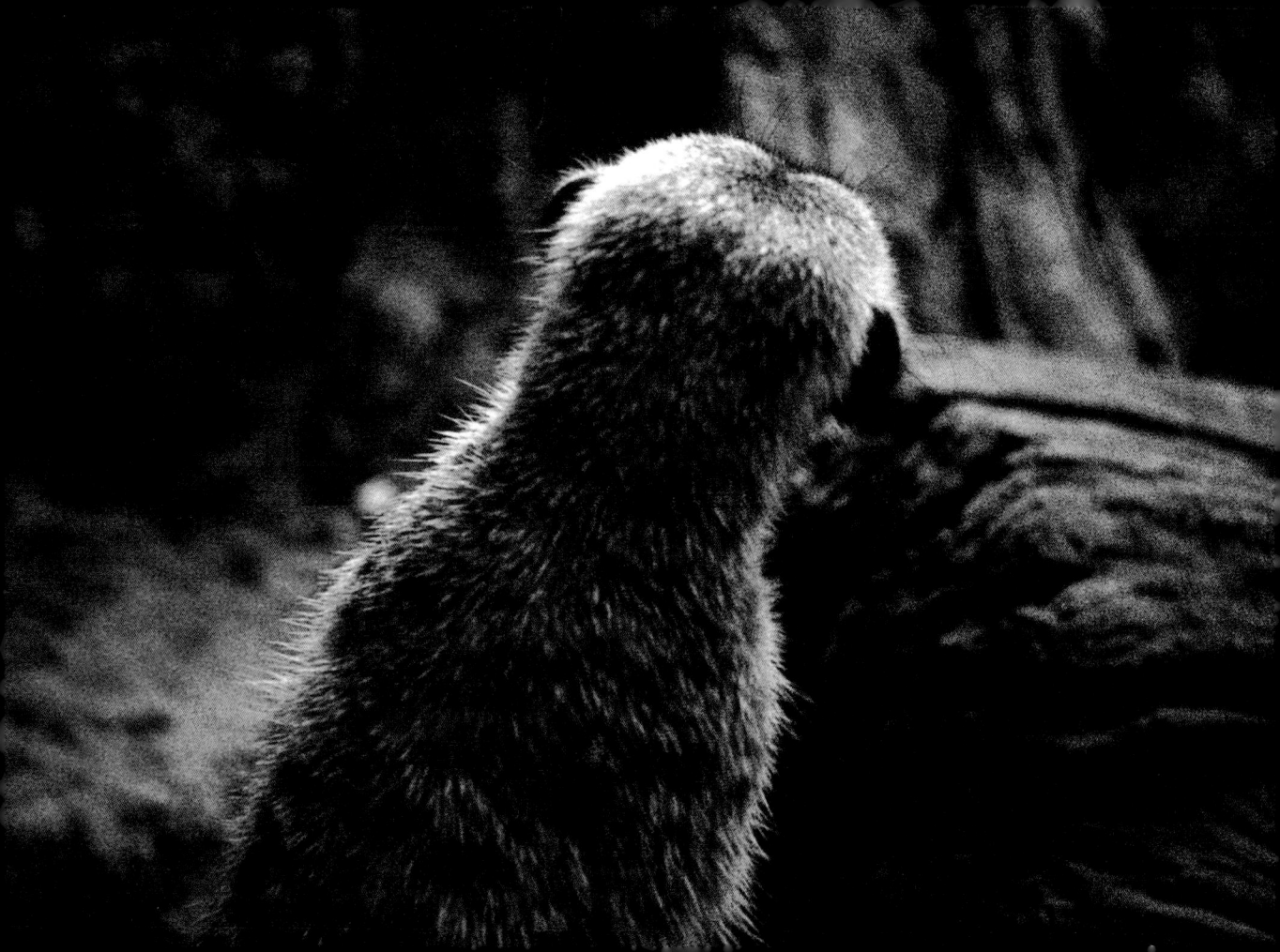

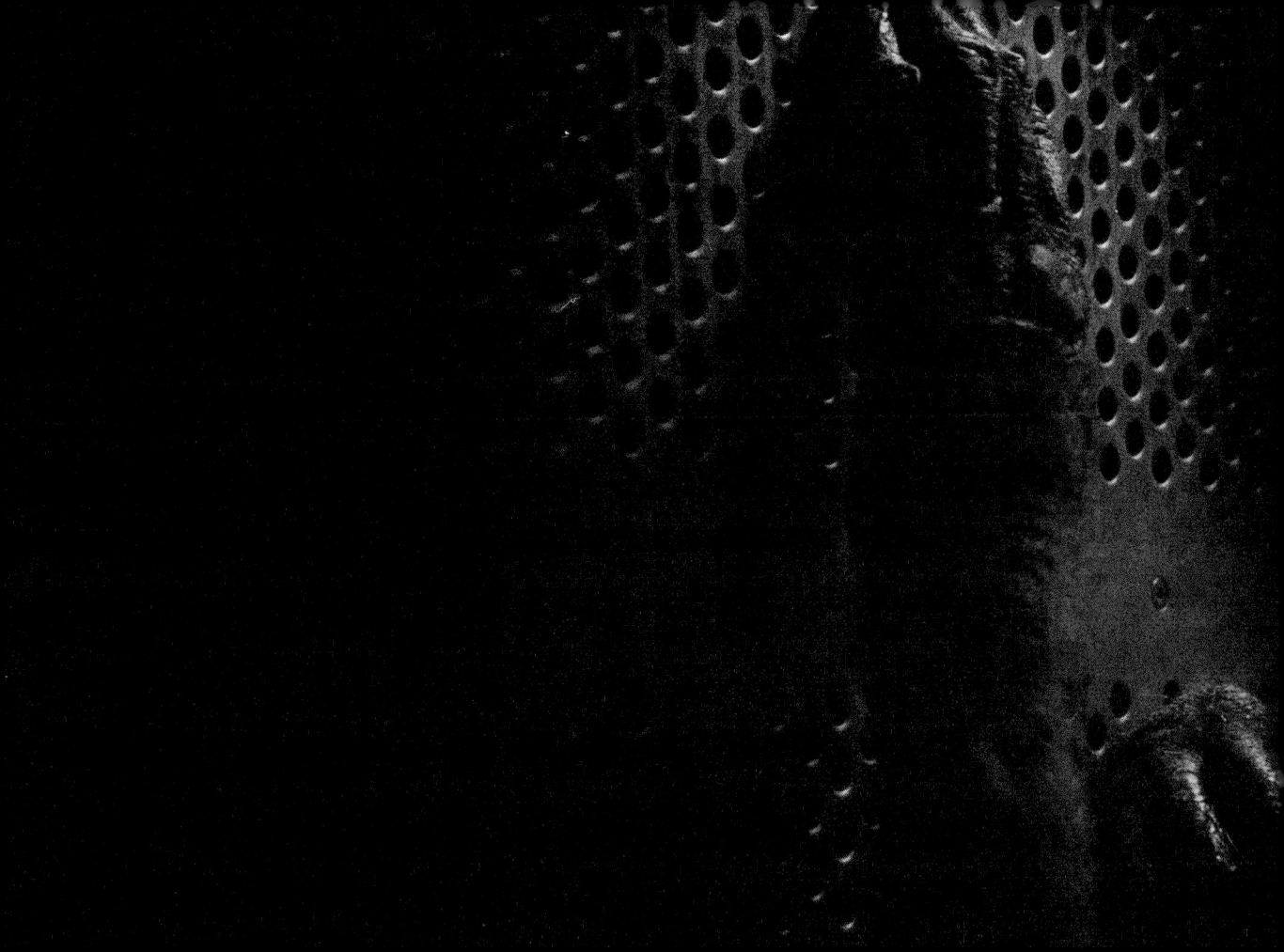

57. Berlin 1992

58. Hamburg 1994

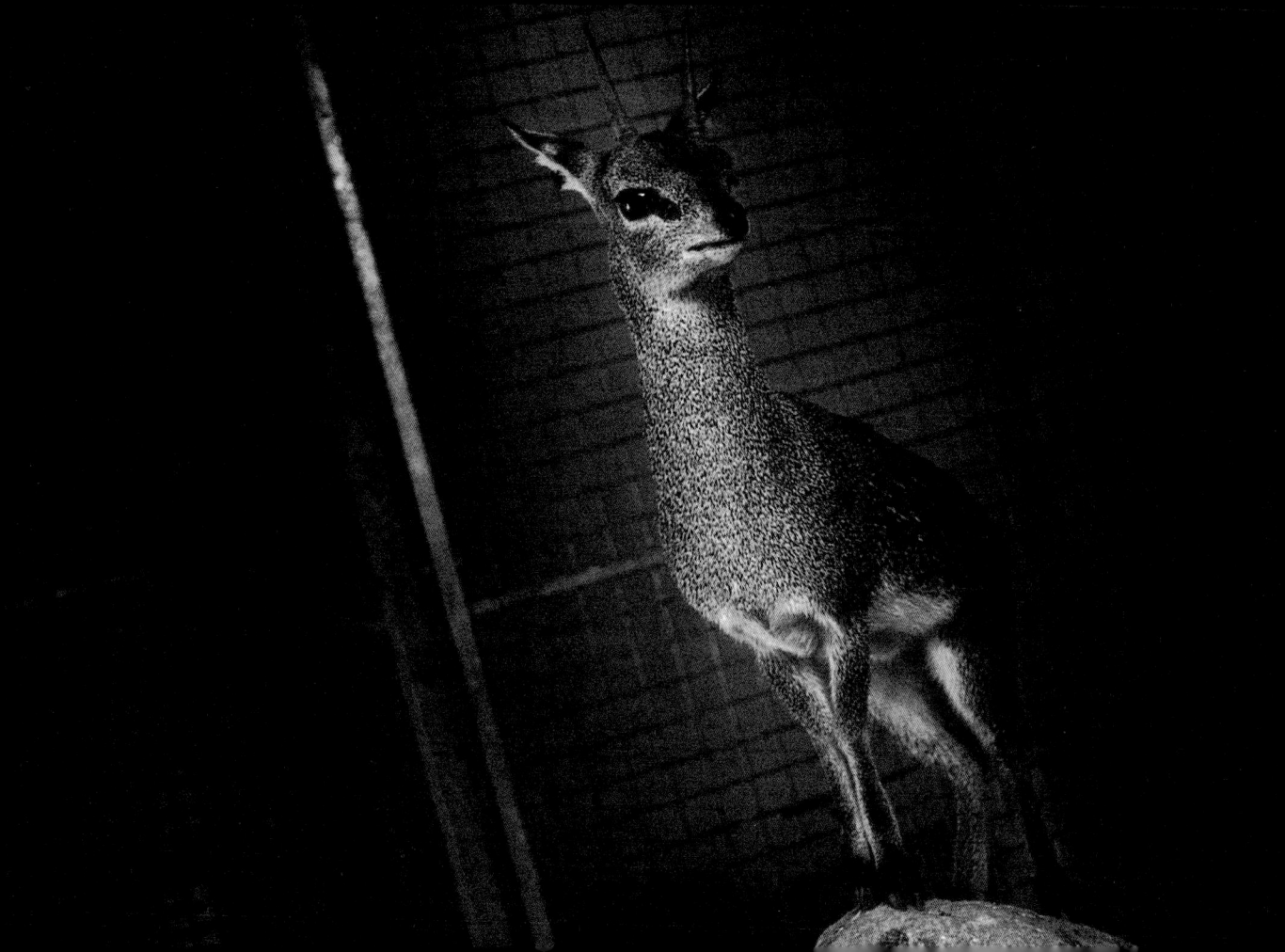

59. Hamburg 1994

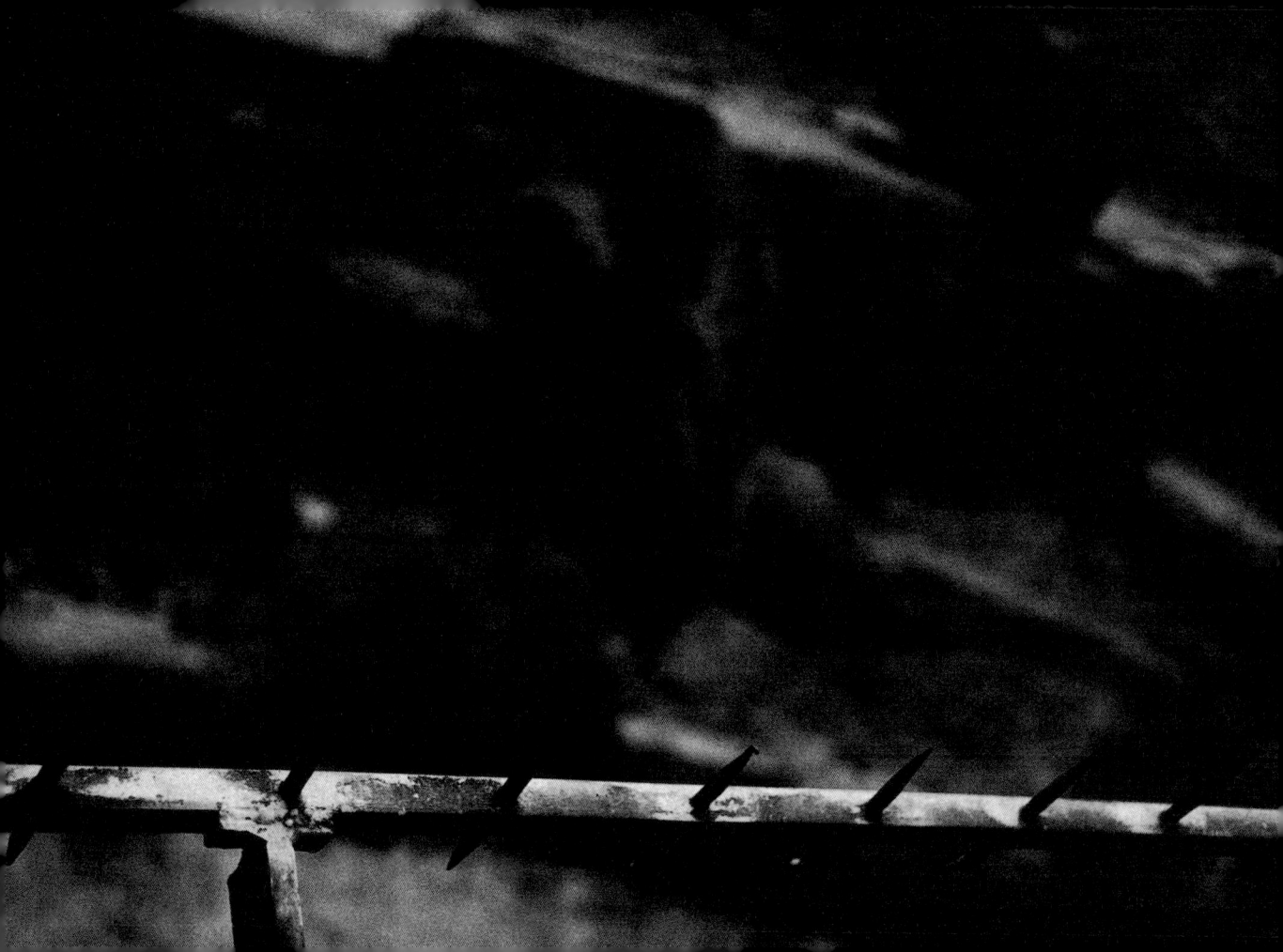

60. San Diego 1995

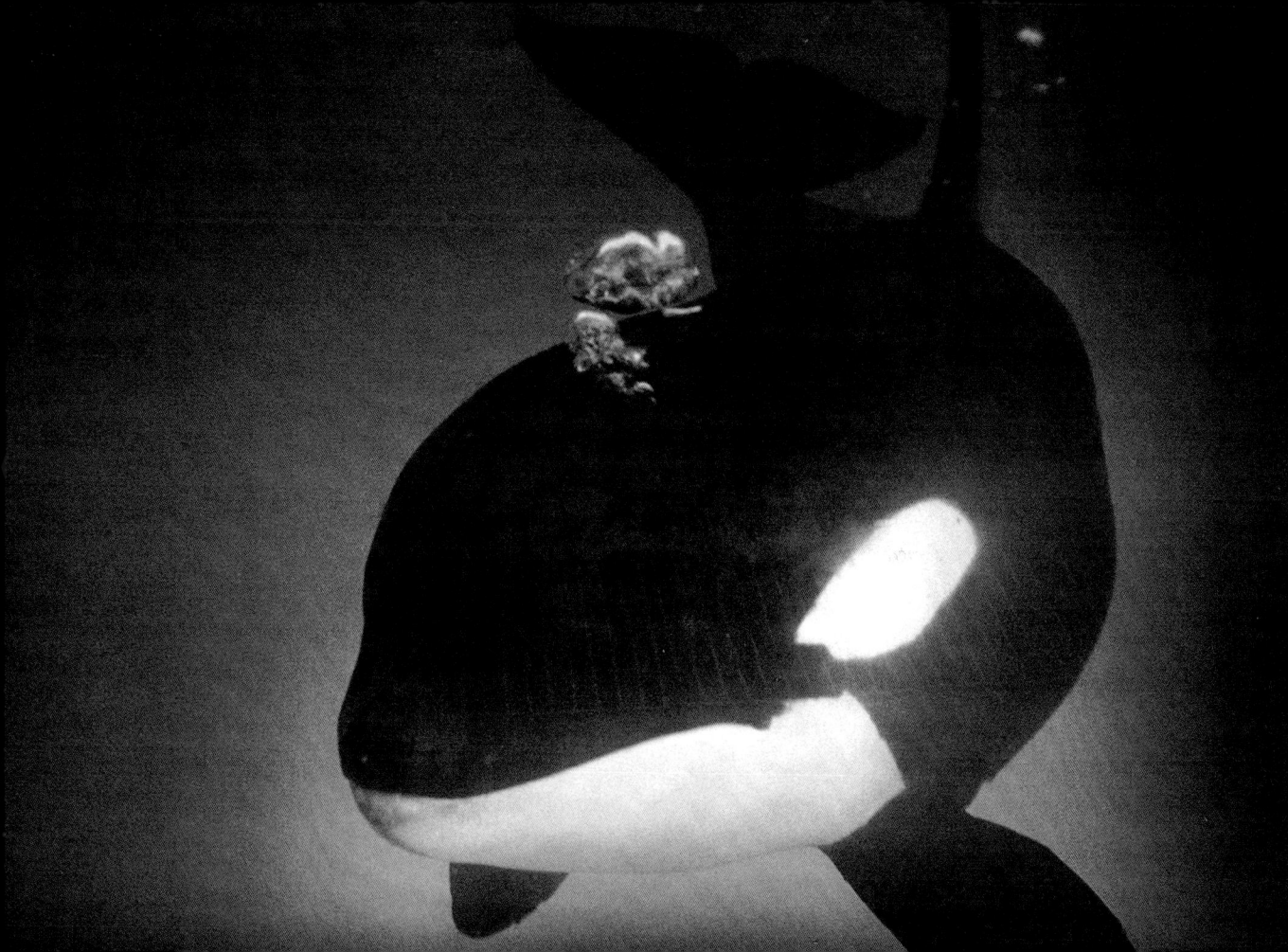

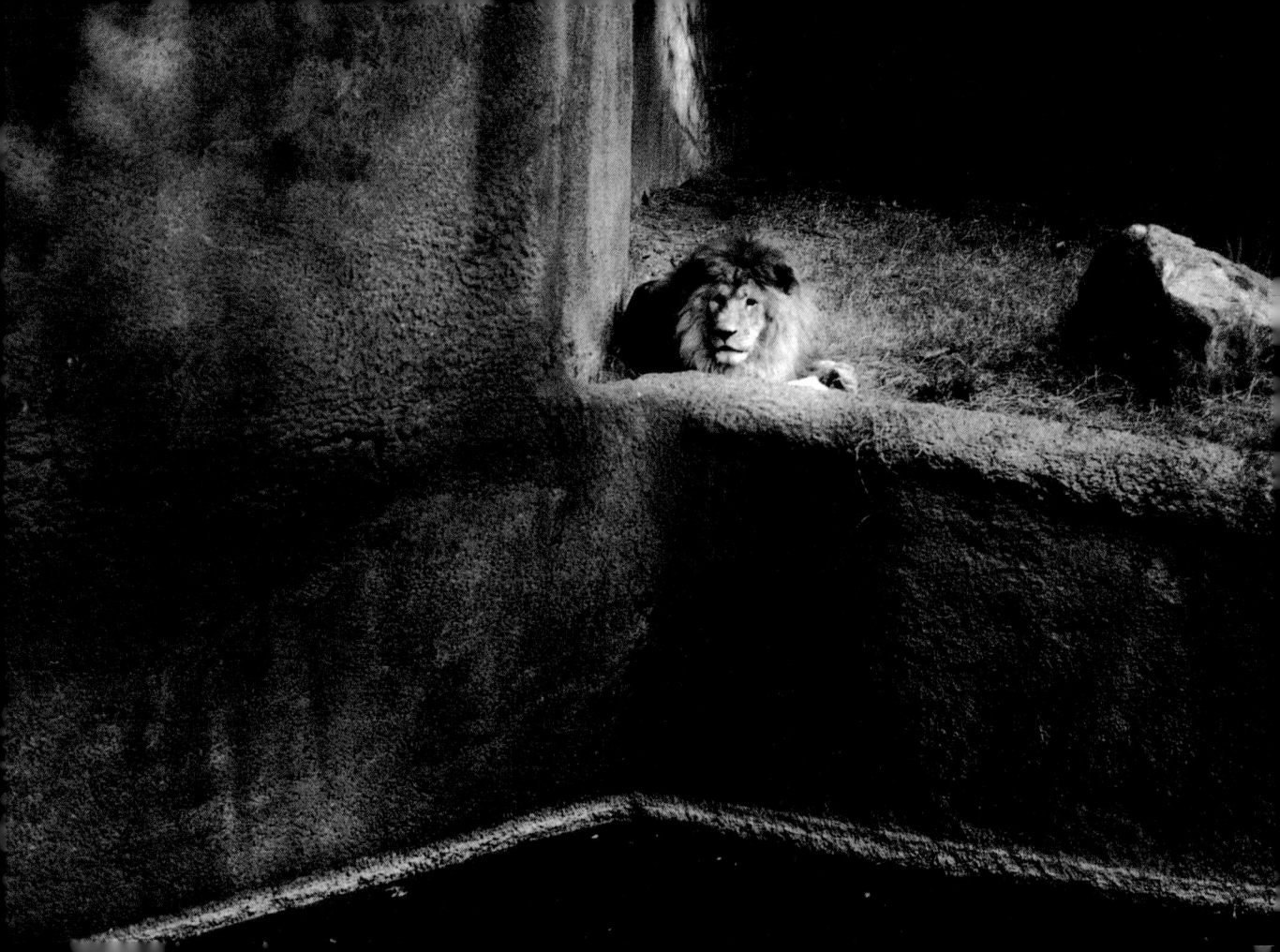

61. Los Angeles 1995

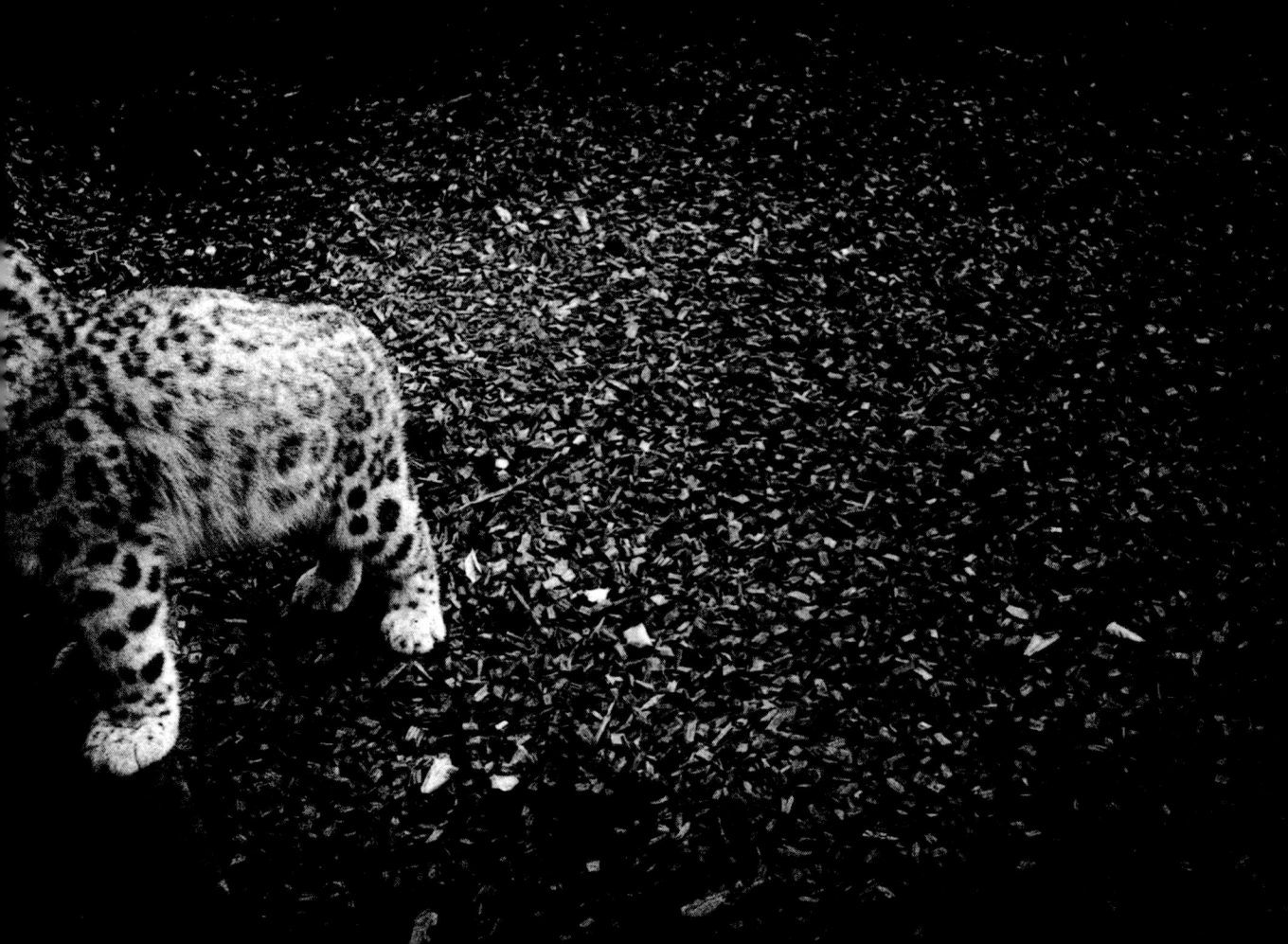

62. Chessington 1994

63. Los Angeles 1995

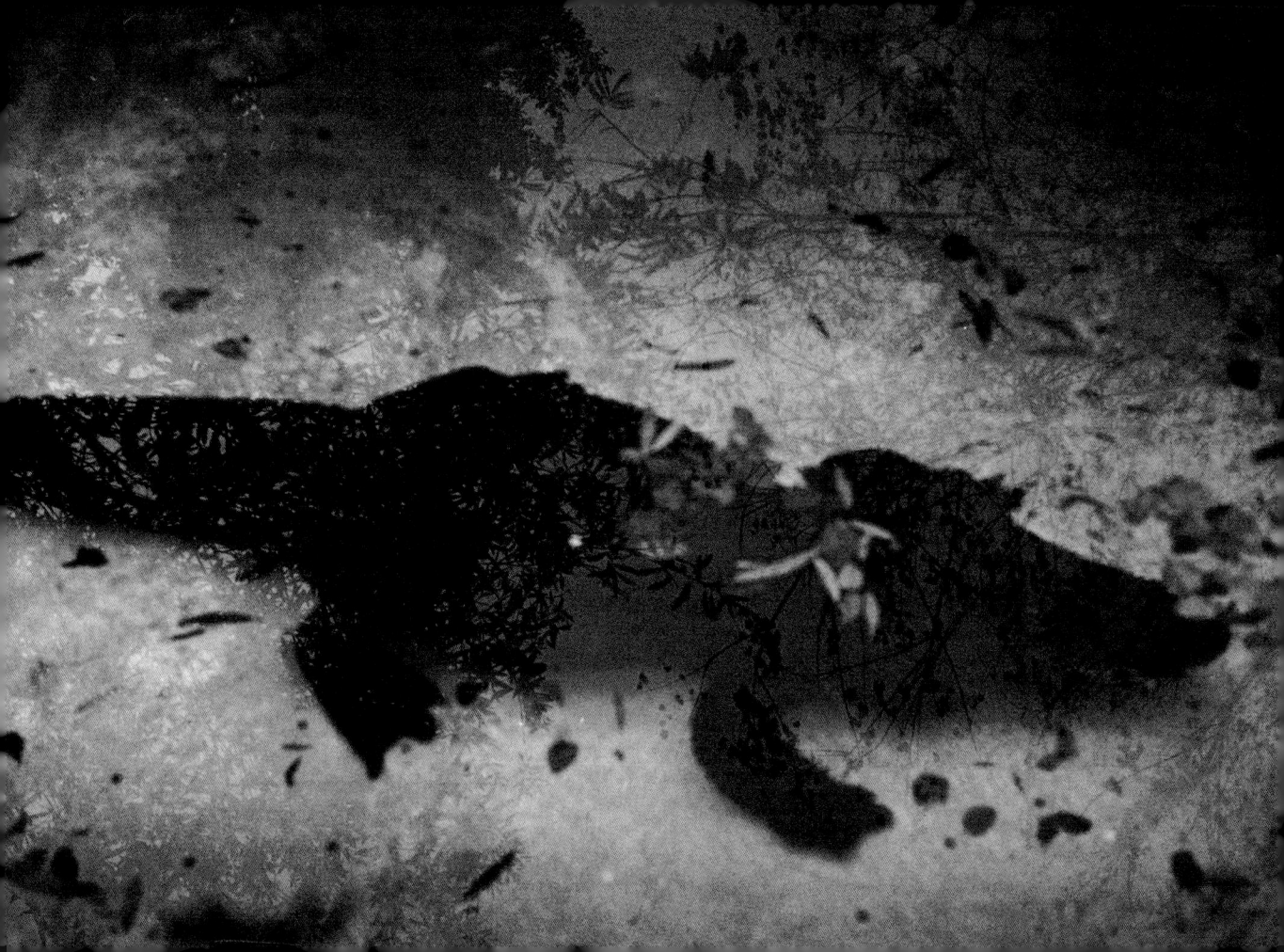

64. Winchester 1994

65. London 1994

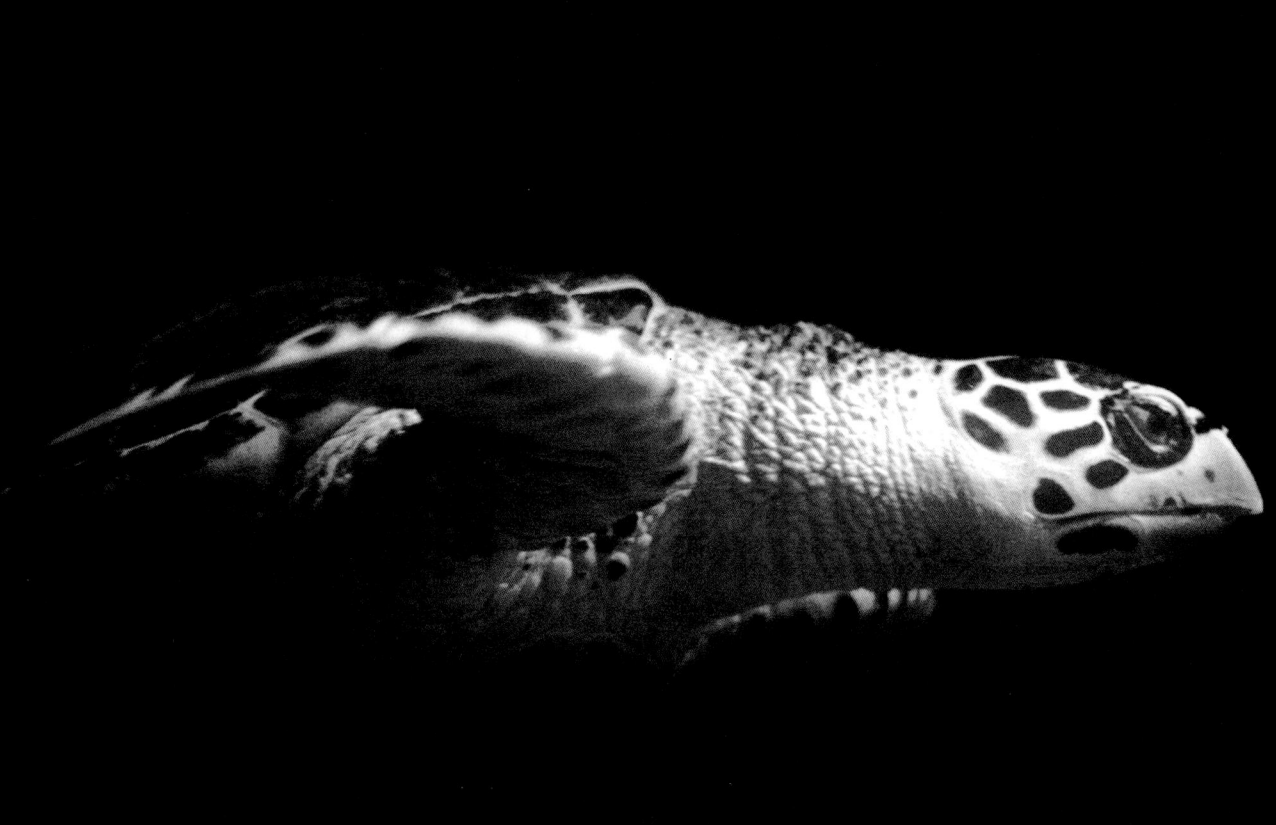

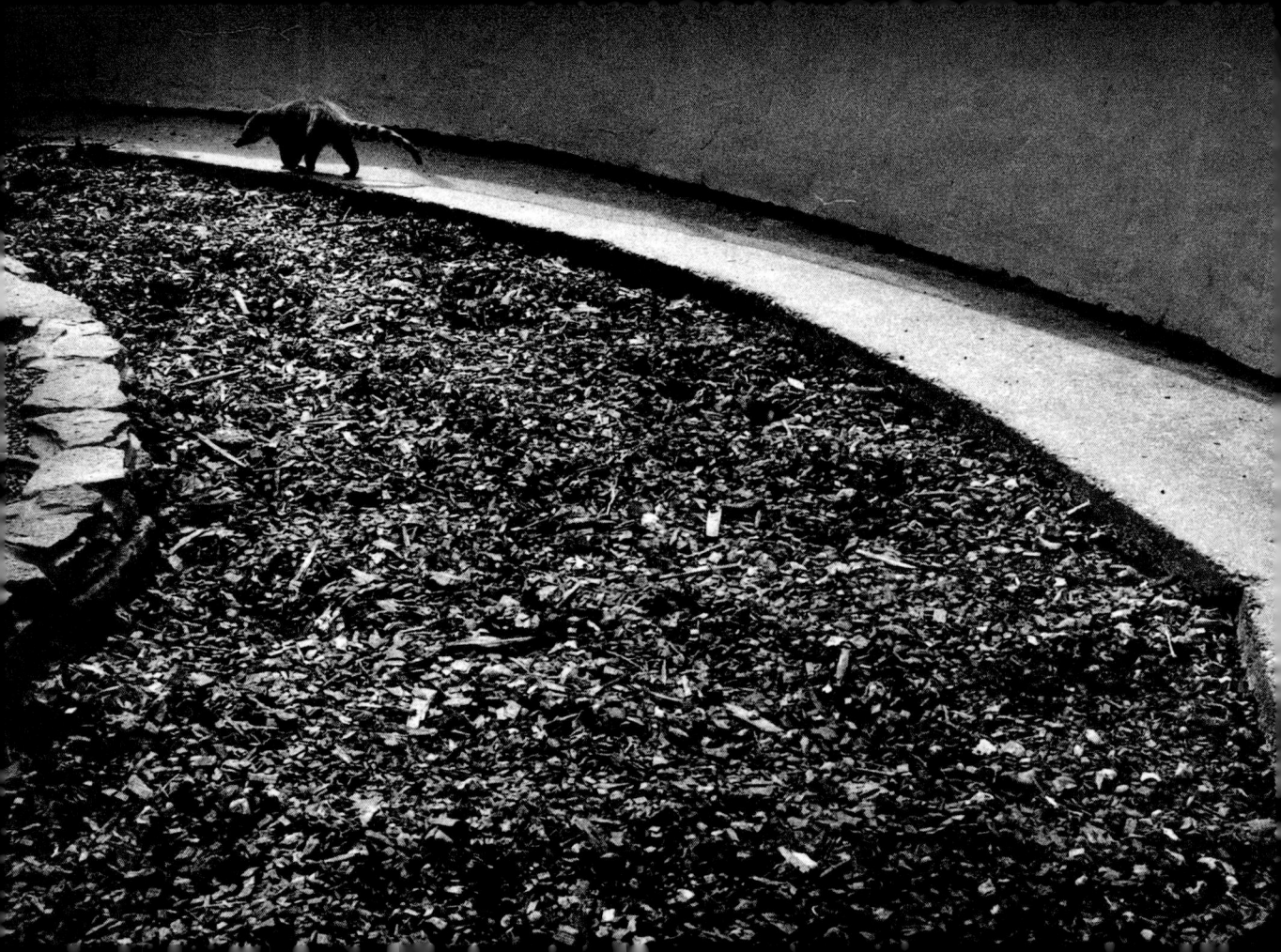

66. Winchester 1994

67. Münster 1994

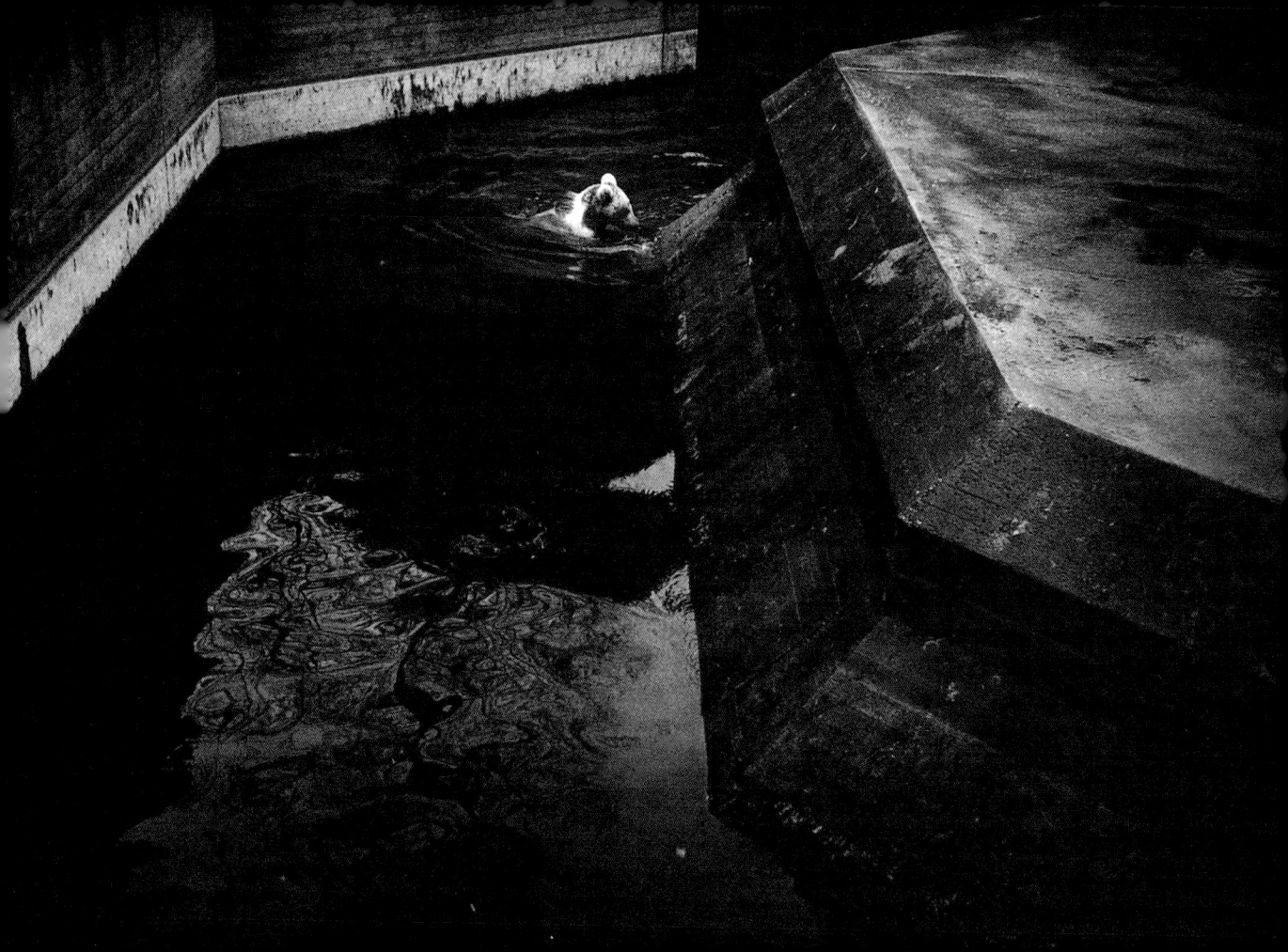

68. London 1992

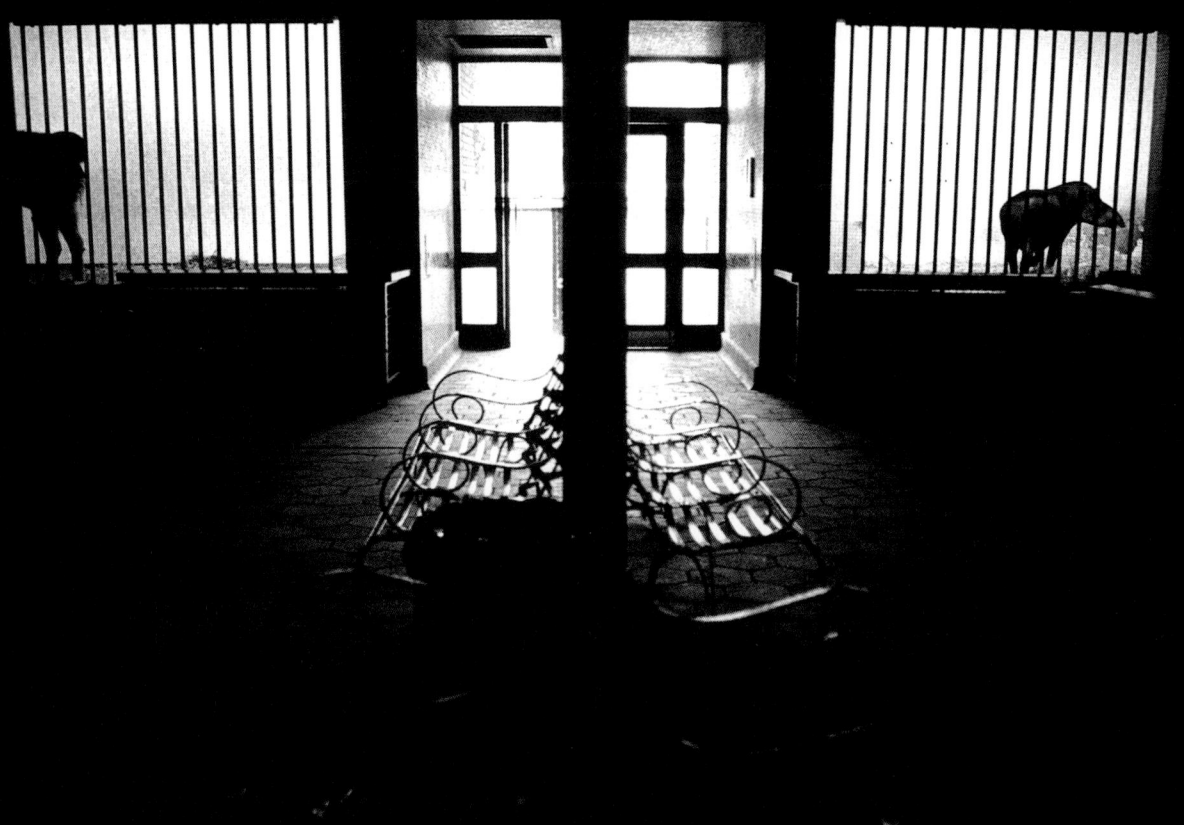

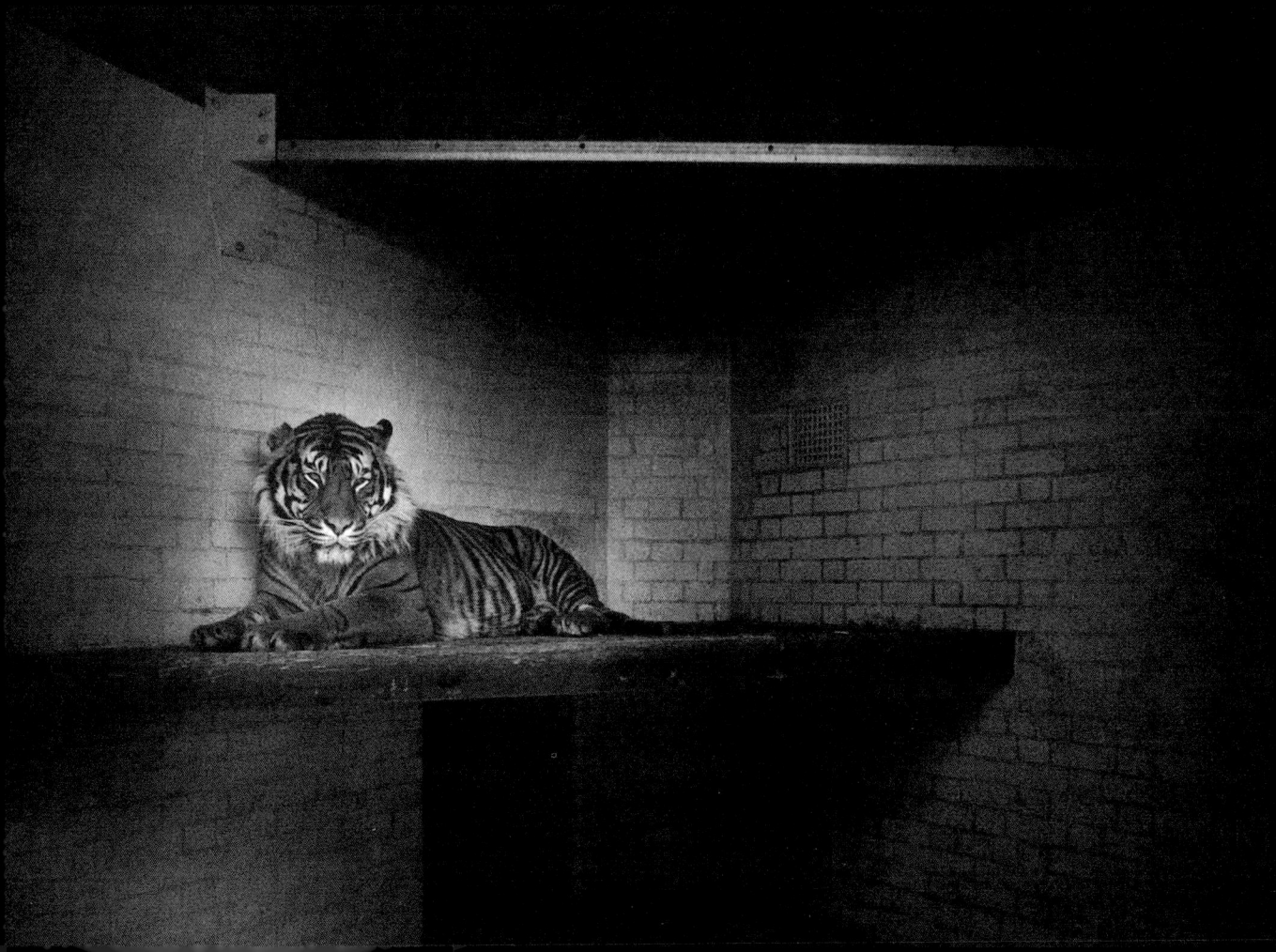

69. London 1993

70. San Diego 1995

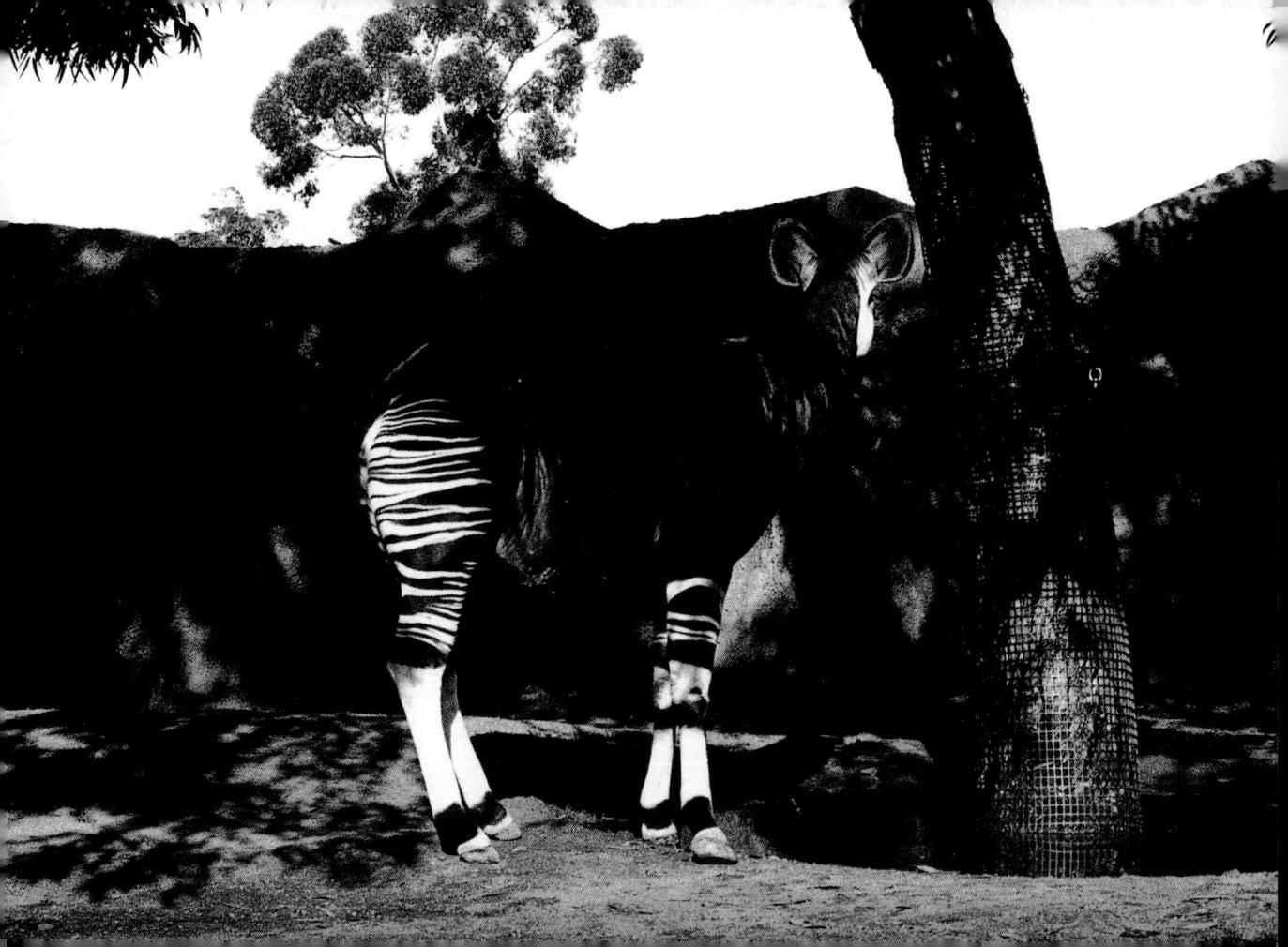

71. Münster 1994

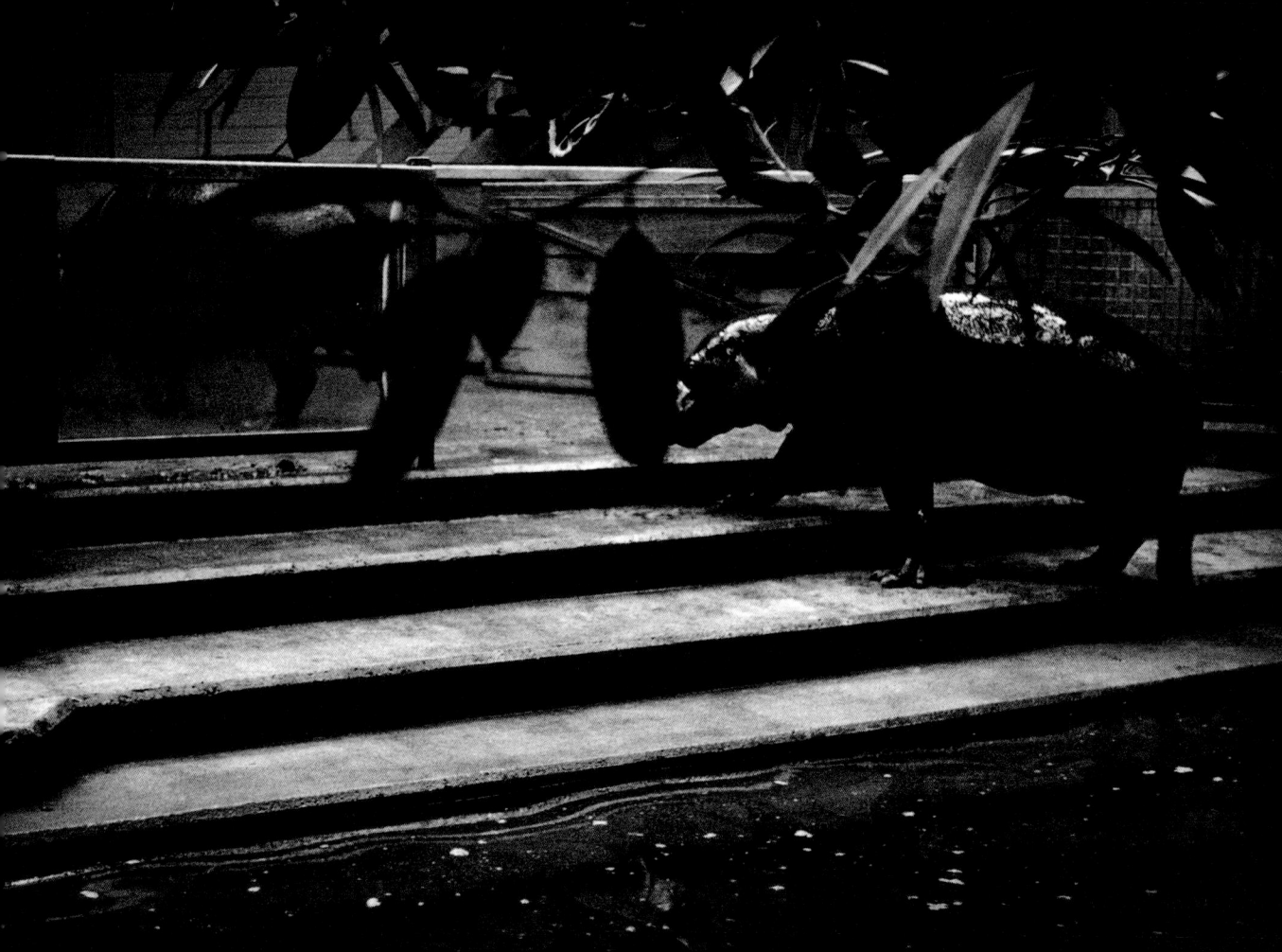

72. Hamburg 1994

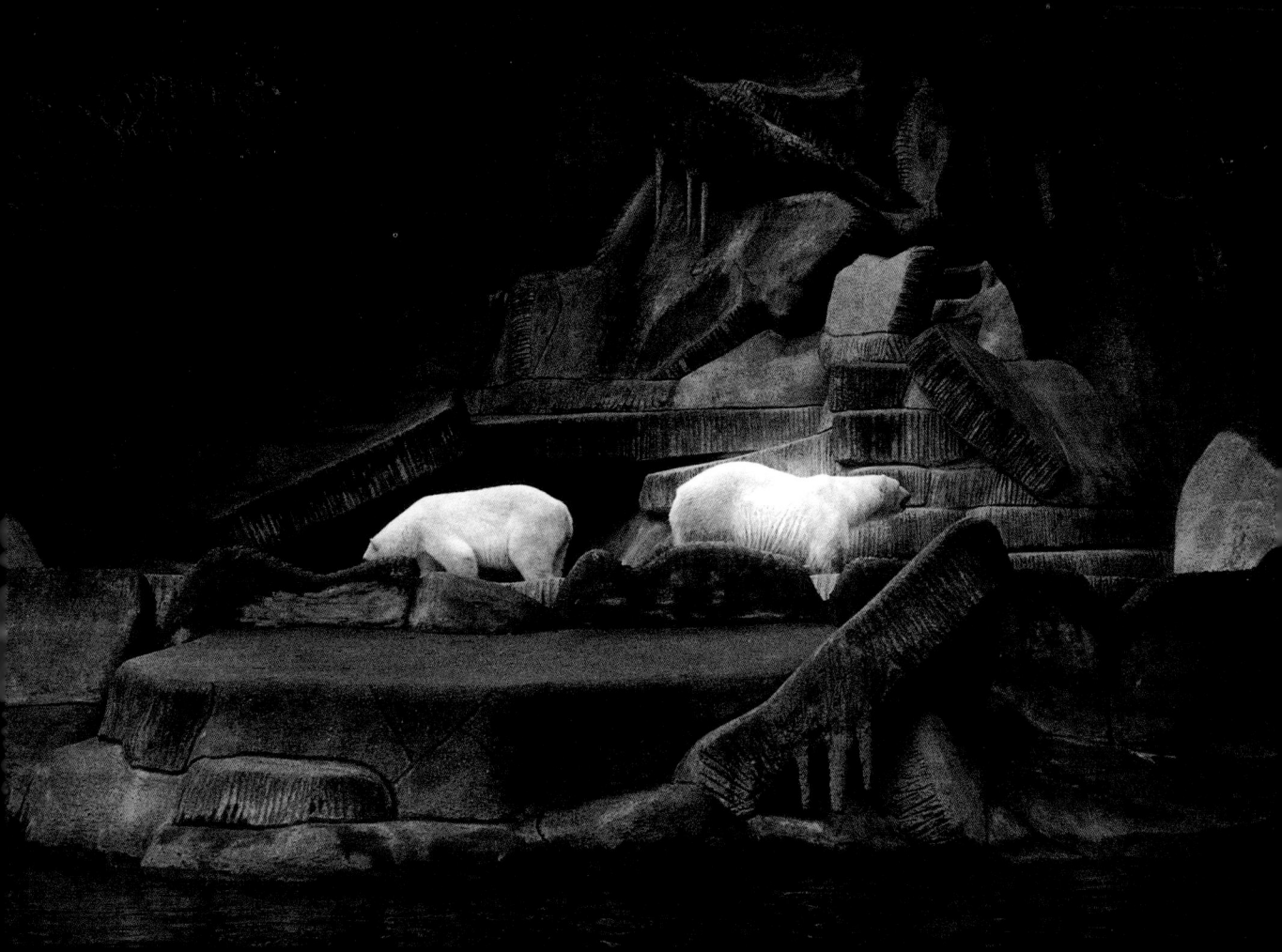

73. Paris 1995

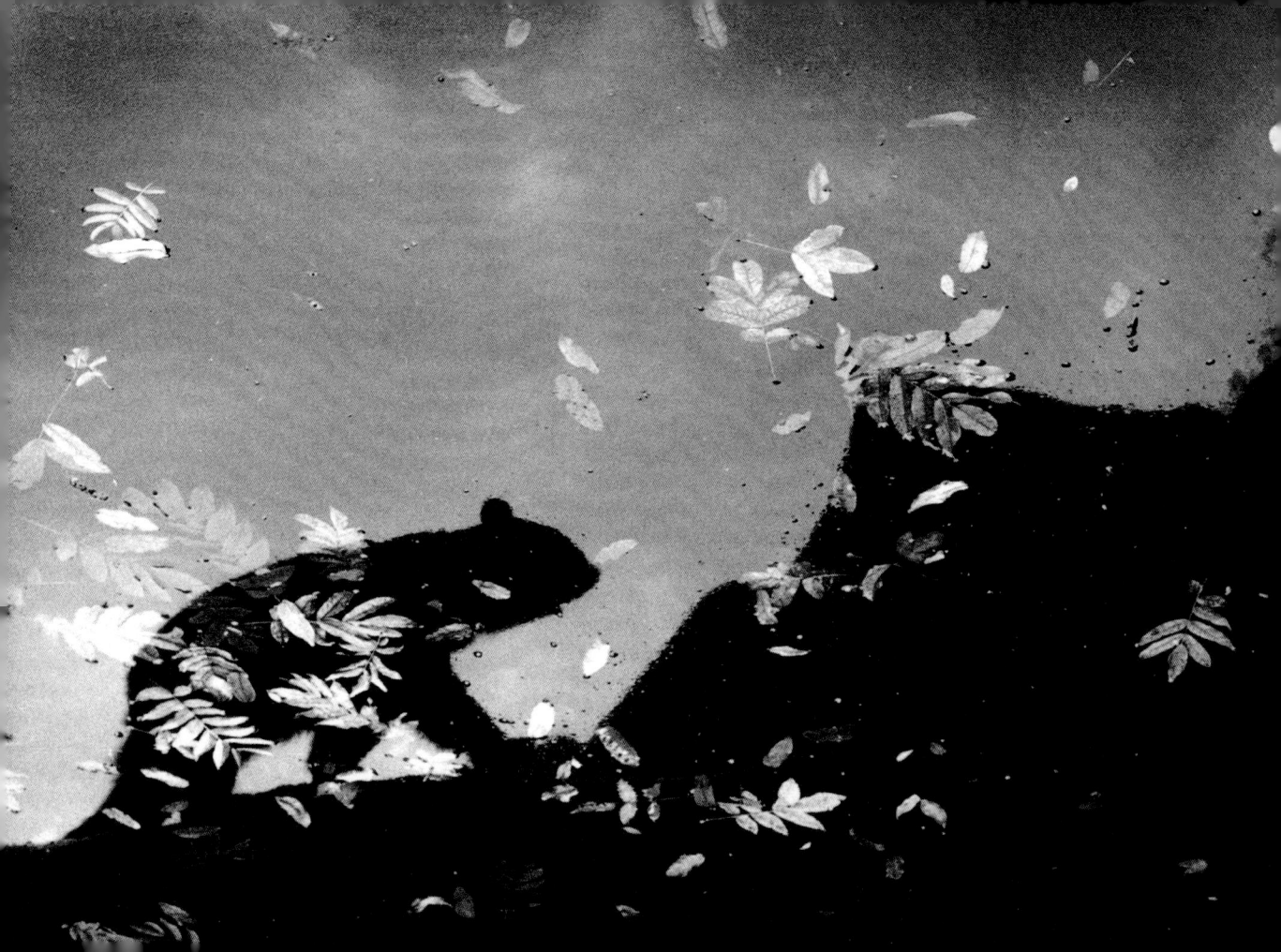

74. Hanover 1994

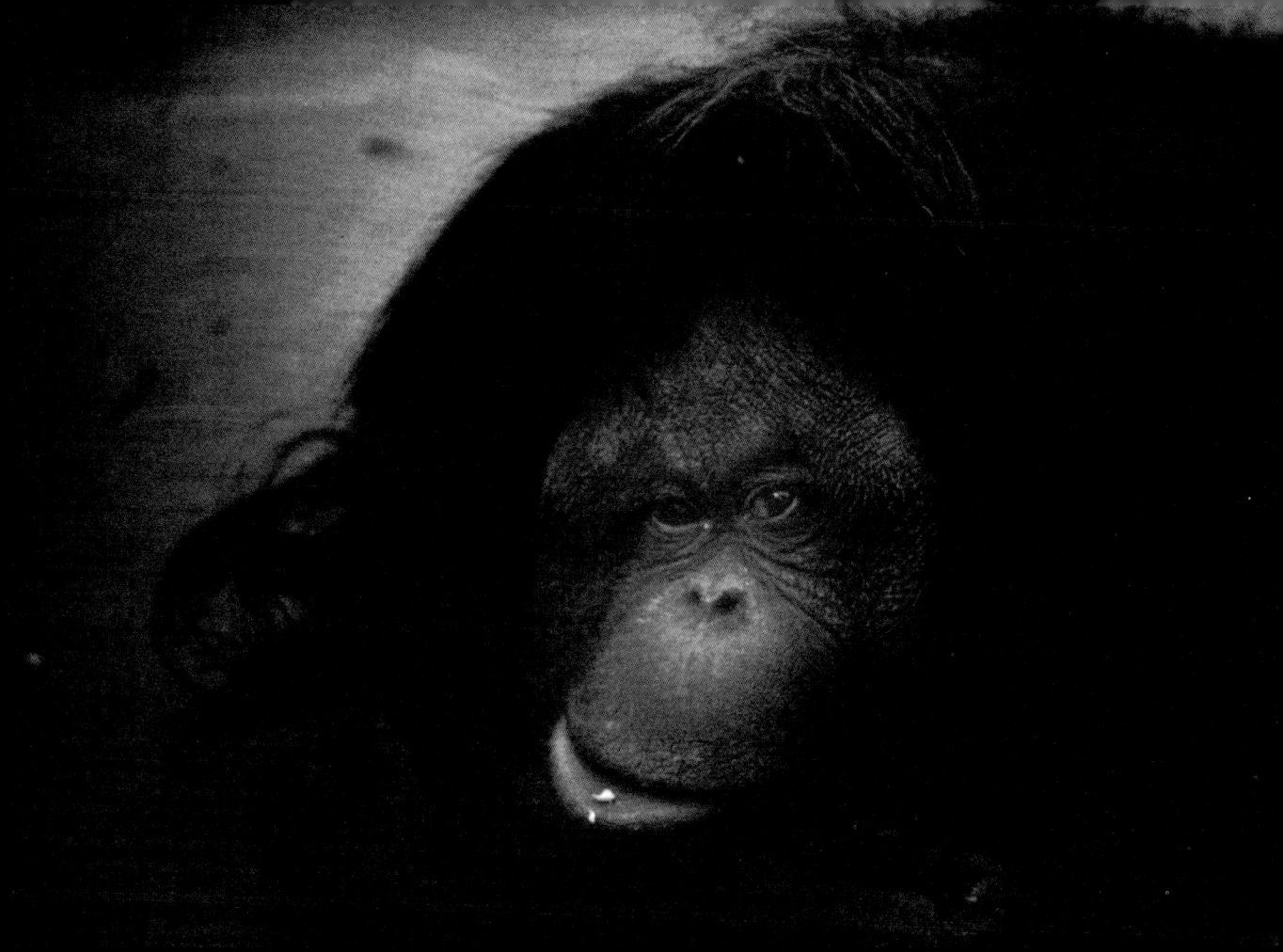

Postscript

I felt it as a child. It was some indefinable feeling, a sense of hopelessness staring out from behind the glass. Perhaps as children, standing on the brink of understanding, we have all felt a vague embarrassment. It may be that we instinctively recognize the unnatural minutiae of incarcerated life or the abnormal behaviour: perpetual pacing, bar biting and swaying. In the end the big event, the ice cream and the novelty of new sights and smells wins out. Eventually, on our progress to adulthood, that malaise recedes and ossifies in the recesses of our awareness. What remains is a kind of primitive regret.

I see children climbing on frames in playgrounds, on the steel and concrete artifice of the human environment and I am not surprised that we project our tastes and appetites onto other animals. It seems absurd to think that toys and hanging car tyres for monkeys or larger concrete cages for wild cats, could replace the Serengeti or the boughs of the rain forest.

It could be that we are unwittingly serving our own appetites. Toys for animals aid and abet our own pleasure, satisfy our own needs, while we pay lip-service to zoos as educational establishments. Adequate information is thin on the ground and what there is, those forlorn blurbs hanging beside The Beast, seems to condescend to both sides of the divide and perhaps illustrate how far we have missed the point.

I feel distinctly uneasy in confined spaces and there is no way of telling to what degree this feeling is a conditioned one or whether it is innate, waiting to be triggered by certain experiences. Whatever the cause, those enclosures still seem to be the expression of our hubris and compulsions, and my grim empathy with the animals enclosed may well have been created out of the dark and fetid corners of these enclosures.

The uneasy paradoxes inherent in zoos have led me to discover aspects of myself, the animals and of a society that feels a need to confine. A stream of emotive, social and psychological associations have swept through my lens and it is precisely because of the complexities, that I would never wish my images to be didactic or even complete. They cannot illustrate but do seem to embody those strains of unease which I – and perhaps many of us – feel. The intention is to allow shades of interpretation, so that if any of my feelings, impressions and ways of seeing reflect some truth, it will be recognized by the viewer.

This work is not a finite project. It is fluid and it is ongoing. It is profoundly important to me and it is also pivotal to all my other work. My images have encompassed zoos but there are no boundaries and there are no ultimate judgements. What there is, within this work at least, is a sense of respect, an acknowledgement of sentient beings whose inestimable beauty and nobility reflects something of ourselves and now, more than ever, lies quivering at our feet.

Britta Jaschinski

Species

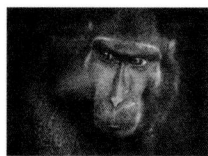

Cover
Chessington 1994
Black macaque
Cynopithecus niger

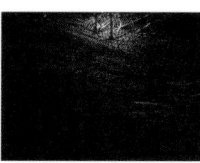

5. Hammerhead stork
Scopus umbretta

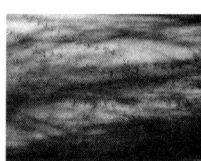

10. Footprints

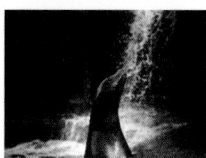

1. California sea lion
Zolophus californianus californianus

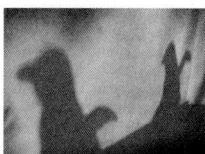

6. Black-footed (jackass) penguin
Spheniscus demersus

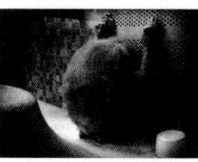

11. Orang utan
Pongo pygmaeus

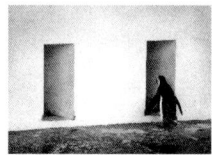

2. Black-footed (jackass) penguin
Spheniscus demersus

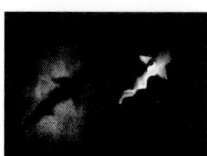

7. Brown shark
Chondrichthyes sp.

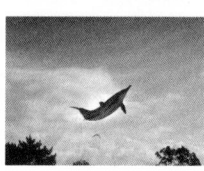

12. Spinner dolphin
Stenella longirostris

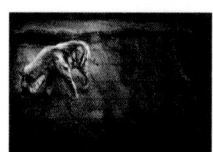

3. Striped hyena
Hyaena hyaena

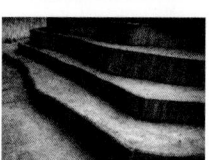

8. Monkey enclosure

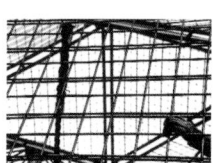

13. Orang utan
Pongo pygmaeus

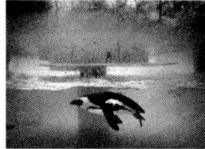

4. Black-footed (jackass) penguin
Spheniscus demersus

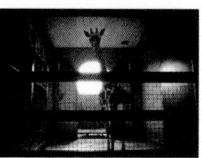

9. Giraffe
Giraffa camelopardalis

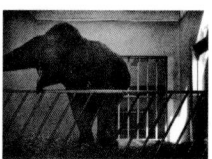

14. Asian elephant
Elephas maximus

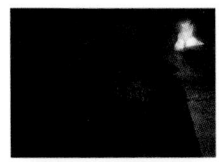

15. Polar bear
Ursus maritimus

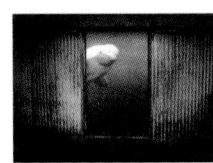

20. Beluga whale
Delphinapterus leucas

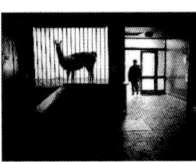

25. Llama
Lama glama

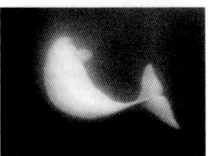

16. Beluga whale
Delphinapterus leucas

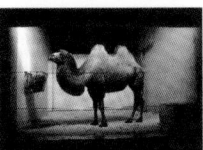

21. Bactrian camel
Camelus bactrianus

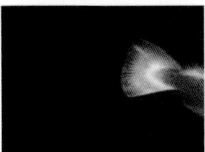

26. Fish fin

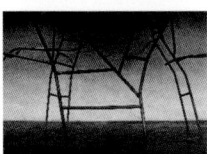

17. Orang utan playground

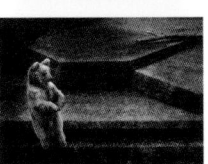

22. Syrian brown bear
Ursus arctos syriacus

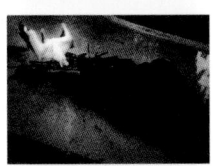

27. Stork
Ciconia ciconia

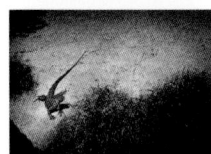

18. Green iguana
Iguana iguana

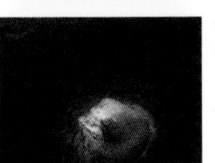

23. Walrus
Odobenus rosmarus

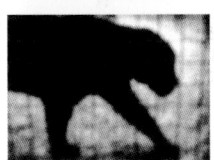

28. Black panther
Panther pardus

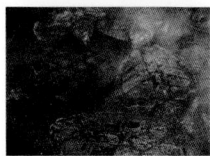

19. Hawksbill turtle
Eretmochelys imbricata

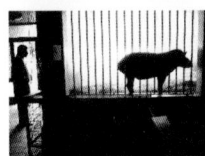

24. Malayan tapir
Tapirus indicus

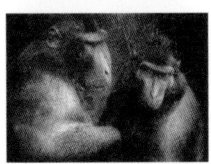

29. Black macaque
Cynopithecus niger

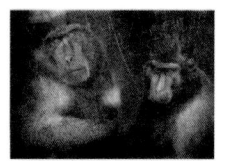

30. Black macaque
Cynopithecus niger

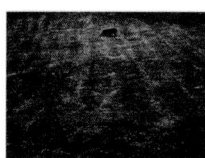

35. Pygmy hippopotamus
Choeropsis liberiensis

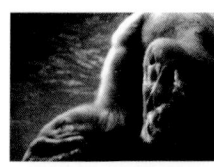

40. Polar bear
Ursus maritimus

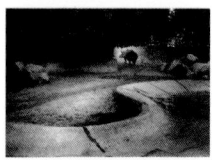

31. Indian rhinoceros
Rhinoceros unicornis

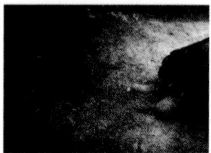

36. Seychelles
giant tortoise
Testuda gigantes

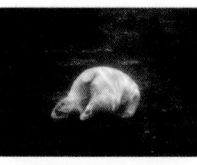

41. Polar bear
Ursus maritimus

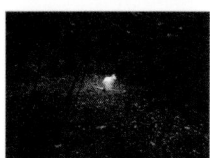

32. Bennett's wallaby
*Macropus rusogrisus
frutica albina*

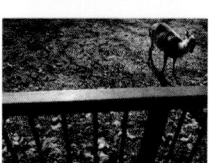

37. Unidentified

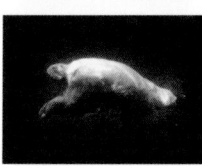

42. Polar bear
Ursus maritimus

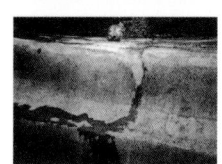

33. Common seal
Phoca vitulina

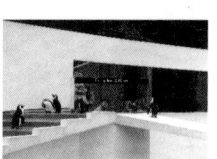

38. Black-footed
(jackass) penguin
Spheniscus demersus

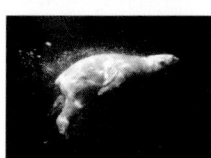

43. Polar bear
Ursus maritimus

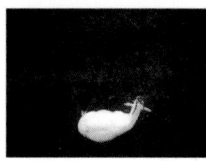

34. Arabian oryx
Oryx leucoryx

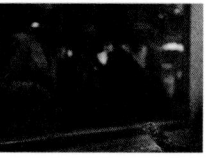

39. Unidentified

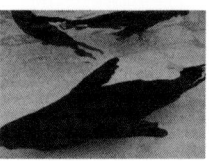

44. Sea lion
Otaria flavescens

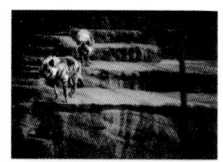

45. Striped hyena
Hyaena hyaena

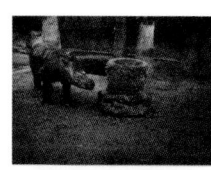

50. Sumatran rhinoceros
Dicerorhinus sumatrenis

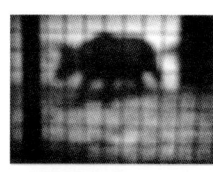

55. Kongo buffalo
Syncerus caffer nanus

46. Steps

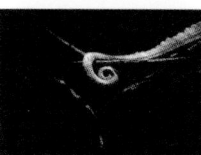

51. Common chameleon
Chamaeleon vulgaris

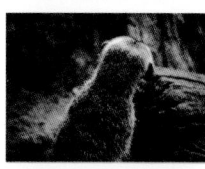

56. Grey meerkat
Suricata suricatta

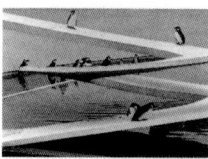

47. Black-footed (jackass) penguin
Spheniscus demersus

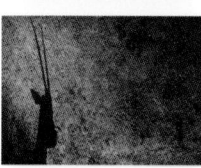

52. Arabian oryx
Oryx leucoryx

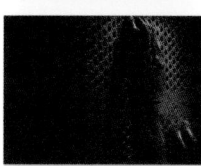

57. Orang utan
Pongo pygmaeus

48. Footprint

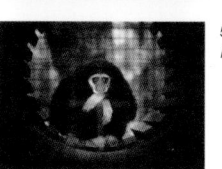

53. Lar gibbon
Hylobates lar

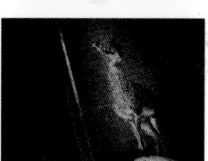

58. Klipspringer
Oreotragus oreotragus

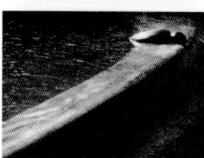

49. Common seal
Phoca vitulina

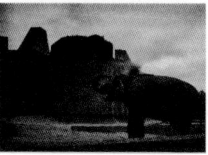

54. Asian elephant
Elephas maximus

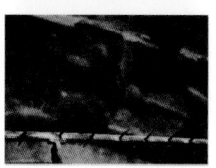

59. Grizzly bear
Ursus arctos horribilis

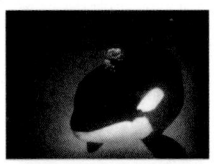

60. Killer whale
Orcinus orca

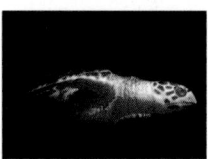

65. Hawksbill turtle
Eretmochelys imbricata

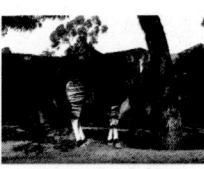

70. Okapi
Okapia johnstoni

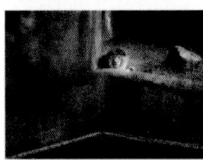

61. Lion
Panthera leo

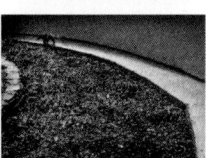

66. Ringtail coati
Nasua nasua

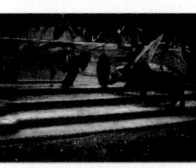

71. Pygmy hippopotamus
Choeropsis liberiensis

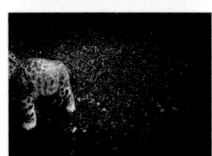

62. Snow leopard
Panthera uncia

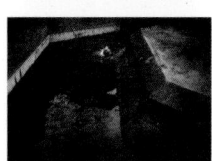

67. Syrian brown bear
Ursus arctos syriacus

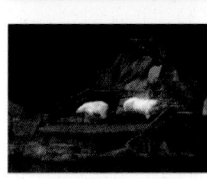

72. Polar bear
Ursus maritimus

63. Alligator
Alligator mississippiensis

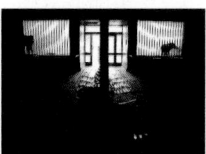

68. Llama
Lama glama

Malayan tapir
Tapirus indicus

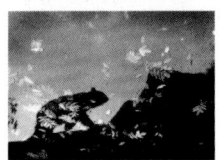

73. Reflection of bear

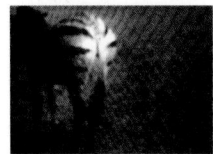

64. Mountain zebra
Equus zebra

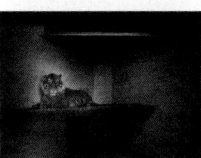

69. Sumatran tiger
Panthera tigris sumatrae

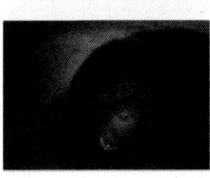

74. Bornean orang utan
Pongo pygmaeus